It Was Inte

50 years as an investigator

Chris Peterson

Table of Contents

Dedication

Jack Giroud, Detective 3 Los Angeles Police Department
"Mr. Robbery"

Acknowledgements

Diana, my wife, my partner and the person who made the book understandable.

Ron Horton, friend, creative consultant and final editor.

To all police officers for their service to each other as well as their service to the public and society in general.

About the Author

Chris Peterson grew up in rural Washington State, graduating from WSU with a degree in Police Science. He joined the Air Force and spent time on a Turkish Air Force base as a Captain in the security police. From there he spent 26 years at the Multnomah County Sheriff's Office retiring in 1997. He has been an established Private Investigator since then. He currently resides in Washington State with his wife, 2 donkeys, a horse, 2 dogs and a pond full of fish.

Preface

The following pages will provide a vivid glimpse into the real world. You will read about sheer moments of terror and friendships that are eternal. There are hundreds of stories and experiences you won't read about, such as the case of a victim, disemboweled, lying dead in a parking lot. I will also skip the story about the mother who drowned her newborn baby in the bathtub. The stories from my career as a law enforcement officer and private investigator are endless, and some can be tedious. Thinking about many of these memories can bring tears to my eyes. Police work can be a tough business in many respects.

My experience with cops was mostly positive. A few of them were crooks. Some had drinking problems or substance abuse issues. Some were lazy, others more aggressive and forceful than necessary. We may have grown tired of the person who decided to spit in our face. We may not have wanted to hear in detail what some fool was going to do to our wife. We may have overreacted when we saw criminals taking advantage of hard-working people. Is there any perfect profession or professional? Probably not.

When I was in college at Washington State University in Pullman, I saw an ad for the drug company McKesson and Robins, looking to hire investigators. This kindled my interest, and the thought stayed with me. The following chapters will show you where that interest led me for the next fifty years. Although I served in the U.S. Navy and Air Force during and after my time in college, I always knew that my true interest was in law enforcement. After my military service was finished, I joined the Multnomah County Sheriff's Office for the next twenty-six years. During this time, I worked in uniform, as a detective, and undercover.

As a uniformed officer on patrol, I always made a point of getting out of my prowl car and mingling with bar owners and patrons, migrant workers and their children, and the community in general. Sitting in the police cruiser and waiting for a radio call was not a successful way to go about the job. Instead, it separated officers from the very people they were sworn to protect. I have mentioned spending a lot of time in bars and restaurants. Those times were some of the most productive in my career. I learned to hear what was going on and made friends with the people who lived and worked in my district. Some of those folks I met during this time were close friends for many years after I retired.

One of my favorite "joints" in SE Portland was the Flower Drum. It was the most popular country western bar with live music in Portland. Ray Lukich was one of the owners. I got to know all the help in the "Drum," as it was called. Ray became my "Uncle Ray." At least, this was how I referred to him. There was a corner bar stool earmarked for me whenever I was there. For many years I saw Ray weekly, sometimes more often. We became fishing and hunting buddies. Ray had live music and dancing at the "Drum." When he was looking for a new band, he would often ask me to go with him as he listened to possible options around Portland. Those trips were always an adventure with "Uncle Ray." This is another example of what law enforcement can look like.

During one of my more memorable trips with Uncle Ray, we were hunting pheasants in Eastern Washington. My wife Diana came to join us for a couple of days. Ray thought I was getting more shooting because my dog, named "DOG," was working more in front of me. Ray turned to Diana and said, "You are going to be my flushing dog, and I am going to call you 'Fred.' Now get out there and start scaring up birds." Forty years later, all of my best friends still refer to my wife as "Fred."

Early on in my law enforcement career, there were several cases that involved Spanish-speaking individuals. I developed an interest in the language and would even hone my skills by speaking with local Mexican families and their children in my district. These incidents sparked my interest in speaking Spanish more fluently, and one opportunity came through community policing as well. I had met a man named Mike McGettigan and his lady Sherry when their stereo store in Portland was burglarized. After retrieving Mike's stolen property through our investigation, he invited me down to Baja, Mexico, for a fishing trip. Over the years, I continued to visit him down there, sometimes bringing my wife Diana along.

Since our early visits to Baja with Mike and Sherry, we have made dozens of trips to Mexico. Several of these were for language schools, one of our favorite spots in Puerto Vallarta, otherwise known as P.V. I think about my times with waitstaff, bartenders, and cabbies or taxistas. Being a friend to these folks produced the same effect as it did at home. I learned a lot of the backstories of Puerto Vallarta tourists and residents: some good and some not so good. All of these stories aided me in my career as a private investigator, as many of my cases involved serving papers or locating American citizens who had fled to Mexico. Once again, this is what law enforcement can look like: community policing on either side of the border.

The chapters that follow are a retrospective of my life in law enforcement. They include an overview of my childhood and adolescence, my time in the military, my early days as a uniformed patrol officer, my time as a detective, my days working in the undercover dope unit, and my more recent work as a private investigator. Some of these stories are amusing, while others are tragic. What follows is a glimpse into the world of law enforcement through the eyes of someone who has experienced it from several different perspectives. I hope you find it as interesting as I have for all of these years.

PART I

Chapter 1

CLARKSTON: CHILDHOOD - 1962

In retrospect, it seems like I grew up in Mayberry, the picturesque fictional town from *The Andy Griffith Show*. My earliest recollections start in "The Valley," where the Snake and Clearwater Rivers come together. This area is formally known as Clarkston, Washington, and Lewiston, Idaho. When I was growing up there, a kid could ride a new bike on Christmas Day in shorts and a t-shirt sometimes. In the early '50s, no one locked the doors to their homes. Kids could be outside well after dark, and at Halloween, we could go trick or treating without our parents worrying we would be poisoned or abducted.

FAMILY

I had the most wonderful extended family that one could hope for. My uncles, Holly and Jesse, were both WWII vets and worked in the local lumber mill. My aunt Dorothy worked in Adam's Drug store on Main Street in Clarkston. She could sell you any number of fascinating items to a child's eye or make you a chocolate milkshake at the soda fountain, where you could sit and visit with your friends for hours.

Grandma Spence made the best fried chicken in the world, and her huge cinnamon rolls were to die for. She was also the Queen of the Clarkston Garden Club, and her yard reflected the love she had for people and beautiful plants. On May days, when I was young, I would pick flowers from Grandma Spence's yard and take bouquets to all the neighbors, and at Christmas time, I delivered them her beautiful holiday pastries.

My father was a school teacher and farmer. During WWII, he spent four years as a navy officer in the South Pacific. He was a wonderful dad, and he taught me what was right and wrong, never wavering from his strong religious beliefs. He could not go to the Fourth of July fireworks without suffering from "Shell Shock," as it was called at that time. Today his condition is called P.T.S.D. It was a reflection of what he and thousands of soldiers and sailors like him suffered as a result of that terrible war. This was the group of people called the "Greatest Generation" by Tom Brokaw.

Being a curious child, I would rummage through any decrepit old building to see what surprises could be found. I searched the beaches and nearby rivers for artifacts like arrowheads and pestles. While rummaging through an abandoned building in an Idaho ghost town, I found one side of a wooden box labeled "Swamp Root." Printed on the other side of the box was "Kidney, Liver, and Bladder Remedy." Even medicine was simpler then.

In my early teens, our family left "The Valley." For three years, we moved to Firth, Idaho, where my father grew up. My grandfather Chris Peterson was a well-known and successful cattle rancher in the area. As a young man, riding horses and helping during round-ups was a wonderful experience. In the Summer, we herded cattle to the nearby mountain ranges, and in the Fall, they were herded back to the ranch. Horses taught me to cut calves from the herd and get them to a spot where they were branded, castrated, and vaccinated. In 1957, I could ride my horse to school and tie him up to the hitching rack out front like people park their bicycles today. I did this on many occasions.

Chris Peterson
Picture was published in the Idaho Farmer

Grandpa Chris Peterson, Idaho, 1950's, on his ranch.

HOMESTEADING

My father, by virtue of his military service, would be eligible to homestead a large parcel of land if selected in a lottery. His name was drawn, and he was awarded one-hundred-and-sixty acres of sagebrush about six miles from Richland, Washington. He arrived in 1958, essentially broke, with an old Diamond T truck and a small Model A Farmall tractor. Our family consisted of four kids and two adults, and our home was a twenty-four-by-forty-foot basement in the desert. There was no running water for the first year. All the water used in the house came down the stairs in gallon jugs.

Being a teenager, I quickly thought the experience was an adventure. I soon got a horse named Sun, and the exploring began. With no fences in most directions, I could ride Sun for miles, and the only thing that got in my way was a tired butt or a thirsty horse. Since we had little money for equipment or help, my father and I scraped all the sagebrush off the land by dragging a large steel beam behind a Farmall Tractor. We would rake the sagebrush up with a hay rake and burn it. The coyotes howled at our fires as we burned at night.

The desert home was a difficult place to live, particularly so for my stepmother with younger children. They moved back to "The Valley," and dad and I stayed on the land, turning it into a successfully irrigated farm that blossomed in the desert. This farmland today is covered with beautiful homes, mini ranches, and a strip mall. The value of the land has certainly changed over the years. So much for selling too early.

HIGH SCHOOL *HAPPY DAYS*

After the desert adventure, dad and I went back to Clarkston, where I finished my last three years of high school. I took up with all my old friends again. It was hot rods, bird hunting, and avoiding the local police as we ran around in our fast cars with the occasional beer hidden somewhere. My pal Duane had a cutoff switch in his car, so he could turn off the tail lights when needed. It really was like the television show *Happy Days.*

Clarkston is unique in so many ways. It is surrounded by near desert hills to the North. On the highest of these hills is the painted "C" for Clarkston. On a lower hill in the same direction is the painted "L" for Lewiston. The average annual precipitation is seventeen inches in the valley. Thus those symbolic letters last for many years before they must be refurbished. Each of the local high schools has taken on the responsibility for maintaining these iconic symbols.

One of the more memorable events of my senior year was a beer party out of town in one of those nearby dry ravines. The police apparently got wind of the upcoming event. All of my friends were there, and every one of them got tickets for minors in possession of alcohol. I was a bit late arriving and sensed it was too quiet as I pulled into the remote area. I told my pal Denny Johnson to throw out our bottle. About fifteen seconds after it hit the ground, the police lit us up with their spotlights and searched the car to no avail. We did not get cited. Lesson number one: pay attention to your surroundings and be ready to react. Thus began my investigative and intuitive career.

A newspaper article came out shortly thereafter in *The Clarkston Herald* about all those miscreants who were cited for underaged alcohol possession. My father talked about all the hooligans and was proud that I was not one of them. This would be my second lesson: learn to hold your mud. At the time, dad was building a house next door for Grandma Spence. He asked me if I could bring some friends over after school to help set the walls up. All of my hooligan friends showed up and helped for an afternoon. I had to hold my laughter in when dad told me afterward, "You have the nicest friends."

WORLD'S FAIR

In 1962, just before graduation, five of us went to the Seattle World's Fair in my beloved '52 Chevy. It was one of the highlights of our senior year. My friends were Duane Beck, Keith Sattler, Denny Plunkett, and Lynn Kuehn. One

7

of this group became a dentist, one became an entrepreneur C.P.A., another one rose to a management level with a phone company, and one became a contractor in Los Angeles. I became a cop.

1962 senior trip to Seattle Worlds' Fair

*Denny Plunkett - Walla Walla police station coming home from the Worlds'
Fair senior trip.*

On graduation night, we did the one thing we weren't
supposed to do; we went drinking. My dad found me the next
morning sitting in my car with a towel wrapped around my
head. I assumed he would not see my robin egg blue '52
Chevy parked on the main street if I had a towel around my
head. When I got home, he promptly put me to work with a
shovel backfilling around the foundation of my grandma's
new home as a lesson. This should have been an early
message. If you want to work undercover, learn to fit into
your environment and not be noticed. Sitting in my robin egg
blue car with a towel around my head in a public place was
not a good practice. After several hours in the hot sun with a
shovel, I managed to sneak off and get a nap. My pals, Lynn
Kuehn and Nancy Webster, showed up that afternoon to see

how I was doing. We were all lying in the shade of my front yard at 1332 Sycamore Street. We had hangovers, and I was in trouble. I remember thinking, "Wow, I am all grown up! What am I going to do with my life?" I did not have a clue but said to myself, "I hope it will be interesting."

THE SEEDS OF LAW ENFORCEMENT

I joined the Navy Reserves prior to getting out of high school. This provided me with some direction. My only connection to law enforcement and investigations prior to this time had been dodging the local police and our beloved police chief, Leo Hellings. Mr. Hellings was the Clarkston Chief of Police for as long as I could remember in my youth. He was appointed chief in 1944 and served a total of forty-four years in the Clarkston Police Department.

Well, there were a couple of other minor connections to law enforcement. I loved watching *Dragnet* and *Car 54* on our small black and white TV. I recall Joe Friday and his partner, Bill Gannon, doing surveillance while sitting in their car. They were talking, shelling peanuts, and throwing the shells out the window of their unmarked detective vehicle. For some reason, that looked like fun. Little did I know that I would spend years of my career conducting surveillance on a lot of bad guys. Sometimes I was in an airplane, other times in a car, and sometimes in a van with lots of camera equipment. Another show that inspired me was the *Andy*

Griffith Show. Barney Fife became an American Icon. I spent years joking about the one bullet I had in my pocket.

To this day, I have lots of friends and some family in "The Valley." As an old man, I still visit Clarkston on a regular basis. There is an emotional attachment to that wonderful little town that I do not understand. My dear father is buried in Vineland Cemetery, and whenever I return to Clarkston, I go visit my pop there. Oftentimes I would wander around this hallowed ground. One day, while looking around the cemetery, seeing some of the family names I grew up with, I saw the headstone of Chief Leo Hellings.

This gave me a start, as I realized here was the guy that had given me several well-deserved traffic tickets. Sometime after seeing Leo's grave, I told my friend Denny Plunkett about my discovery. Denny said, "He is buried close to my dad, and Leo is still looking over him." Denny went on to tell me that his dad was a heavy drinker but that Leo had treated him well for many years in spite of his problem. The chief's headstone is in an elevated location at the cemetery. I want to think that the chief is still looking out for all those who admired him for so many years.

Looking back on my youth in Clarkston, I would like to think that Chief Hellings had a positive influence on the course my life was to take. The stories about Chief Hellings are abundant. It was common knowledge that sometimes Leo would give a down and out person a place to sleep in the

High School classmates - 50th reunion

city jail. He would often take money out of his pocket to help those in need. I guess that Leo was Clarkston's, Andy Griffith.

Chapter 2

COLLEGE/ NAVY BOOT CAMP: 1962-1966

In 1962, I went to navy boot camp in San Diego, CA, with a group of my friends. After only a few months on the job, I was the senior sailor in the group. I was charged with everyone's orders and told to make sure we all got to the training center. I was terrified of losing someone. All these years later, I am still in touch with several of those former sailors and friends. After boot camp, I asked for a deferment to attend Clark College, which the navy happily provided.

CLARK COLLEGE

During my freshman year at Clark College in Vancouver, WA, I began wondering what I was going to do for a living. I did my navy reserve drills on a destroyer escort, the U.S.S. McGinty, in Portland, OR. As a signalman, I got to spend most of my time on the bridge of the ship. This was an interesting place to be, as all the steering, navigation, and major decision-making took place on the bridge.

U.S.S. MCGINTY

The McGinty has a special place in my heart. Commissioned in 1944, she was soon in the South Pacific, and in a short time, the ship was involved in preparations for the invasion of Japan. On the way to Hawaii on the McGinty in 1963, I learned how small a destroyer escort could feel when we were in a serious storm. To this day, it is still a thrill to think that I was able to spend time on an American warship that likely had crossed paths with my dad at some point during the war.

W.S.U.: POLICE SCIENCE

In the Fall of 1963, I enrolled at Washington State University in Pullman, WA. I wandered through my second year, finally realizing that I needed to make some choices about a major. Starting my Junior year at W.S.U., I knew a decision had to be made, as the navy wasn't going to give me deferments for the rest of my life. Looking through the catalog of courses at W.S.U., I saw the Police Science section, which only required twenty-nine credit hours in the major. I thought that might work with my delayed decision-making. Having actually started working towards my teaching credentials, a stint at student teaching and collecting lunch money clarified that this profession wasn't for me. I knew that Washington State and Michigan State were the only two universities that were offering these types of courses in the late 60s. Today most junior colleges and universities have some type of criminal justice program.

PROFESSOR FABIAN

When I began majoring in police science, my immediate inspiration was Dr. Felix Fabian, who taught Criminal Law, much of which was derived from English Common Law. Felix was not an attorney, but it was clear that he understood the tenants of criminal law as they might apply to those of us looking at a career in law enforcement. I was immediately interested in the subject and hit the ground running.

During the 1960s, there was a lot of unrest on college campuses. W.S.U. did not get as swept up in the protest movement as many campuses, but it was still there. Dr. Fabian often debated other college faculty members who would be called progressive today. I recall being proud that I now had Felix as a professor and mentor. It was a different time, for sure. Felix would smoke multiple cigarettes during a one-hour lecture. He had been a police sergeant in Texas prior to teaching. His language was interesting and a bit different from all of my previous teachers and professors. This guy got my attention.

PROFESSOR MCCALL

Don McCall was another one of my professors. His educational background was Chemistry. Don taught the courses that involved "scientific investigations." He taught about fingerprint classifications, plaster of paris tire print impressions, and tool impressions left behind by burglars as they plied their trade. Don had been a Portland Police Officer. He was seriously injured on his first day on the job and walked with a limp for the rest of his life. He never worked again as a police officer. Harry Moore, a retired Secret Service Officer, was another professor. These educators were all quality staff.

NAVY O.C.S.

In 1965, the navy sent me to Officer Candidate School in Newport, Rhode Island, for twelve weeks during the summer prior to my senior year in college. I was scheduled to go back to Newport the following summer and complete the last twelve weeks of Navy O.C.S. Those twelve weeks were intense, and I got a glimpse into the duties of a U.S. Naval Line Officer and what my life in the navy would look like. One main thing that I learned from this experience was to always be responsible for my decisions and actions.

Upon returning to W.S.U. for my senior year, I knew my interest was in law enforcement rather than a military career. I hoped to use my time in the navy to channel this ambition in that direction. I spoke with an air force recruiter on campus and told him about my desire to find a career in law enforcement. He suggested the air force, which had the Office of Special Investigations (O.S.I.) Among other duties, the O.S.I. was sort of the air force's version of a detective unit. The navy had nothing even remotely similar to this type of opportunity available, so I chose to transfer military branches. My move to the air force was the beginning of my law enforcement career.

DON CLARK: RECRUITER

Another fortuitous event happened during my senior year, which led me to my career path in law enforcement. Don Clark, who was the youngest person to become the sheriff in Oregon's Multnomah County, visited the campus looking to recruit college-educated folks to be cops. I guess Don accomplished what he wanted to do because I did go to work for M.C.S.O. after the military. Don ultimately became an influential person in the County. He was the Chairman of the County Commission and the Chief Executive of Multnomah County for a number of years.

Chapter 3

MILITARY: 1967-1970

The navy allowed me to switch my enlistment to the air force, but they gave me a drop-dead date. If I wasn't in the air force by the specified time, I would start my two years of active duty as a third-class signalman, which was my navy rate at that time. I accepted this offer and switched military branches from sea to air. Almost as soon as I was sworn into the U.S. Air Force, they told me there was not a position open in O.S.I. They suggested flight school as an alternative. Although the flight tests came easily to me, being a pilot was the last thing that I wanted. Nevertheless, I was sent off to twelve more weeks of O.C.S. training with the air force in San Antonio, TX, even though I knew that law enforcement was my destined path.

Officer Candidate School was becoming old hat, as I had a lot of practice by this time: navy basic training, navy O.C.S., and now air force O.C.S. There were fourteen hundred candidates in my class. As we neared graduation, an instructor asked the fourteen-hundred of us if anyone was scheduled for flight training that did not want to go. I raised my hand. During a pleasant conversation with an air force major who was a pilot, I told him that I had been badly misled by the recruiter. My plea fell on deaf ears, and off to flight school, I went. I was there for about twelve weeks and did well in academics, but I did not have any desire to fly airplanes.

SHAW AIR FORCE BASE, SOUTH CAROLINA

The air force found a place for me. They stationed me at Shaw Air Force Base in South Carolina. I was a second lieutenant in the security police squadron. The job involved the security of military assets, policing the base, and liaison with local law enforcement in the civilian community. I then went to San Antonio, TX, for a five-week police academy. This academy taught all the subjects one would expect: firearms, self-defense, report writing, and a myriad of related topics.

SAN ANTONIO AIR FORCE POLICE ACADEMY

Part of this training was to participate in a ride-along with the San Antonio Police Department. Up to this point in time, I had never actually been in a real police car. My view of the world was about to change. Several memories stand out. One of my first stops each night with my new coach was a topless bar. That was interesting for this farm boy from Clarkston, to say the least. Another time, two drunks had been fishing, and one of them got bit by a rattlesnake. His buddy decided that he should bring the offending snake to the E.R., so there would be no doubt about the serpent's species. Of course, the snake got out of the bucket in the E.R., and you can imagine the scene. On a different occasion, I was called to the medical examiner's office one night, and there were all of these six-foot trays that still had human blood on them. Welcome to my new world. I wasn't so sure how I felt about what I was seeing.

There was a local barrio with a lot of violent activity, and everyone there spoke Spanish. One person had a serious stab wound. I had no idea what to do and was dumbstruck by the chaotic environment. As a woman started running from the scene, the officer was up to his elbows in the mayhem. As she ran, he yelled, "Grab that bitch." I did what I was told, but at that moment in my young life, I discovered that my new career would entail more than sitting in a car with Joe Friday shelling peanuts under the shade of a beautiful Sycamore tree. We would routinely meet with detectives for coffee at a local bar or diner. This was when I started to experience the camaraderie and the special bond that existed among law enforcement.

After the air force police academy, I returned to my new home in South Carolina at Shaw A.F.B. As an officer, I was more in a supervisory role than a police officer. My education as an investigator and police officer was about to start. I had master sergeants with eighteen to twenty years of experience in the police and security field working for me.

Most of them had done a number of overseas assignments, including in Vietnam and Korea. Fortunately for me, I had five-and-a-half years as an enlisted sailor under my belt, so I thought that it might be a good idea for me to watch and keep my mouth shut for a while.

The confinement facility known as the brig was located thirty feet from my office. This was my first experience with inmates. Most were not incarcerated for serious crimes, but occasionally there was a real criminal. One of my first inmates was Bobby Greenburg. Bobby was from New York City, and he was addicted to narcotics. At that time, the air force had emergency medical kits placed in areas that were readily available if there was a need for them. All of these kits contained morphine curettes. It became apparent that someone was stealing the morphine. Bobby had some pending legal issues, and he indicated that he could help me with the morphine thefts if I helped him out. This was my first experience dealing with inmates as snitches. It would not be my last. I agreed to help Bobbie, and of course, I learned a lesson very quickly. Bobby was the thief, and we found his stash of morphine when we searched his room in the barracks.

Shortly after my arrival at Shaw, I became the number two officer in the security police squadron, also known as the air cops. There was a lot of civil unrest in the country due

21

to the anti-war movement surrounding the Vietnam War. One of the regular training scenarios involved riot control. Given the fact that we were at war, it seemed such a shame that riot control received so much attention. That was our country in the '60s. Unfortunately, there are a lot of similarities today, as police officers are continually involved with civil unrest and do not have time to deal with routine public safety.

PALMER COLLEGE: CHIEF LES GRIFFIN/ SHERIFF BYRD PARNELL

My duties included liaison with law enforcement in the area. I happily executed that aspect of the job; after all, I was interested in law enforcement beyond the fences at Shaw A.F.B. It was here that I got to know Les Griffin, the chief of police in Sumter, South Carolina. I was also introduced to the sheriff of Sumter County, Byrd Parnell, and his number two man Tom McJunkin.

The local school Palmer College contacted me about teaching classes to law enforcement officers. The goal was to give police officers a formal education that was essentially unavailable in the area at that time. The other instructor was a local attorney who taught criminal law. As flattered as I was, in retrospect, I wasn't in the least prepared to teach veteran police officers much of anything. The lesson I learned here was: never agree to do anything that you are ill-prepared to do.

On my first night as Professor Peterson, who did I find sitting in the front row? None other than Les Griffin, Byrd Parnell, and Tom McJunkin, are the top three police officers in the area. Tom McJunkin had spent a number of years with air force O.S.I. and went to work for the Sumter County Sheriff's Office. He obtained two master's degrees and became a minister upon retirement from law enforcement. My knees got rubbery, and I was trying to think of a way to escape. Thankfully, no one ever threw things at me, and they attended all the classes. One night, Sheriff Parnell approached me and asked for permission to leave early so he could speak to the garden club as he was running for re-election. The sheriff was a court-recognized expert in five areas, and he was asking for my permission to go about his business. This was a humbling experience, to say the least.

South Carolina Police Course "Professor Peterson"

Byrd Parnell was inducted into the South Carolina Law Enforcement Hall of Fame in 2017. He had been elected sheriff in 1952 and served Sumter County until he retired in 1981 with forty-two years of experience. This was the man who was asking me if he could leave class early! Sheriff Parnell was well known for his apprehension of "Pee Wee Gaskins" in 1975. Gaskins was a serial killer believed to have murdered more than one hundred people during his crime spree. Griffin, Parnell, and McJunkin were all great influences on my career.

As I neared the end of my time at Shaw, I applied for a law enforcement job in Portland, OR. I used the sheriff as a reference. He sent a letter to my prospective employer and said, "If you don't hire him, let me know, as he has a job with Sumter County." When I retired from Multnomah County twenty-six years later, I wanted to get a copy of the letter, as it meant so much to me. Unfortunately, our records were not maintained after retirement, and that treasure had been destroyed.

One night as class was ending, Tom got called out on a rape case involving a black male suspect and a white female who was an air force dependent. He invited me to follow him through the investigative process. I had heard about the so-called "racist cops" in the South and was very interested in observing. The suspect was tracked down and arrested in a swampy area. I observed Tom and his fellow officers as they made the arrest and processed the suspect. I had never heard the "N" word once, and I saw nothing but professionalism during this intense evening. Sometime later, Tom and I had a conversation about this case. I expressed my admiration for the episode that I had witnessed and told him that it went beyond my initial expectations. Tom told me that he had grown up with a black "Mammy," and he respected her like his own mother.

During this time in Sumter, one of my airmen was arrested and charged with a minor crime. I was able to follow this case through to trial. One of the detectives who handled the case was Lou J. Degenhardt, who wore a suit and a pair of well-shined wingtips. The Sumter courthouse is a classic Southern building in the town square. Det. Degenhardt was the epitome of a professional while on the witness stand. I thought to myself that I would like to be like Lou when I grew up. Lou was a retired air force major who had been a P-51 pilot in World War II, and he was awarded the Distinguished Flying Cross with Clusters while serving in the European Theatre of Operations.

STATE PEN

At one point, I visited the State Penitentiary near Columbia, South Carolina. I don't recall why I was there, but I do remember an interesting moment. A guard introduced me to a black male inmate who was quite polite and pleasant, but it turns out he was in prison for murder. He had actually been sitting in the electric chair when his sentence was commuted. The inmate told me about his crime. He ended his story with, "I was ready, but they weren't."

CAESAR NAPOLEON PRINCE

Many years ago, *The Readers Digest* regularly featured an article titled "My Most Unforgettable Character." My unforgettable character from Sumter, SC, and Shaw A.F.B. was Caesar Napoleon Prince. Caesar was black and grew up in Sumter. As Caesar was nearing retirement, he was only an

E-4 Sgt. He had not done well with promotions. He worked for me in the security police squadron and was a widower raising three young children. There were instances when folks working for me needed a day job. Caesar got that assignment when I could arrange it. To see him direct traffic at an intersection was poetry in motion. I immediately liked Caesar, and we became fishing friends. This was not the way it was supposed to be. The military wanted officers and enlisted folks to maintain some distance in terms of socializing.

Caesar owned a "juke joint" in Sumter, which was a bar with a predominantly black clientele where a lot of gambling took place. Caesar was always in the middle of it. One day I saw him driving a newer Buick Riviera to work; it was a beauty. I said, "Sgt. Prince, did you buy a new car?" He said, "No, lieutenant, I won it in a card game." This was not anything a boy from Clarkston could understand. Someone wins a newer car gambling? Shortly after this, Caesar got sent to Vietnam. We kept in touch as he continued his gambling enterprise. One day after Caesar and I got out of the air force, I suggested that we go to Vegas together. He implied that his type of gambling might not be a good idea in Vegas. I eventually lost track of him.

Years later, I wanted to find Caesar, so I contacted a bail bondsman in Sumter, as I knew that Caesar had done this kind of work after his retirement. The person I spoke with said Caesar was no longer in that business. Rumor had it that someone had jumped bail, and a bondsman went to the air base and took that person out at gunpoint. I never verified the story, but I'd like to think it was my friend Caesar.

I eventually found Caesar living in Bakersfield, California. He had graduated college with a degree in education and taught school for several years. His two sons were successful in the insurance business in Bakersfield, and his daughter was doing well. Caesar was driving a Mercedes and was hosting gambling sessions at his home. He still loved his Hennessy Cognac. Rest in peace, Caesar.

OFFICERS' CLUB: PILOTS

Shaw Air Force Base had a beautiful officers' club, and I was a regular. There was a stag bar in the club where no females were allowed. My, how things have changed. Most of the patrons lived on the base. Thus the stag bar was the site for a lot of overindulgences. One night the on-duty sergeant from the security police squadron called to request my presence at the officers' club. He said there were two drunk majors acting out of line in the club. It was my first experience with the police being sent to the officers' club over any kind of disturbance.

There were a number of senior officers seated in the dining area with their wives, and I was a bit surprised that none of them had approached the two drunken majors. Neither had two of my security police officers who were on the scene. It seems that no one wanted to get involved with two drunk majors who had over fifty mission crushes in their caps, signifying they had been flying over North Vietnam dodging S.A.M. missiles and other unpleasant flying objects. My experience with drunks was a bit limited at that time. Years later, I knew that there was very little point in trying to reason with drunks. After declining to leave when asked, I handcuffed the two drunken majors and took them to jail.

Later, a nearby neighbor of mine on the base, Colonel Anderson, came up to me one day and said, "Pete, a lot of us liked what you did at the O' club the other night." Pete was a nickname many people have called me over the years, as my last name is Peterson. Unfortunately, there was a general on the base who wasn't so keen on his majors going to jail. Colonel Anderson made this comment to me as I was preparing for my new assignment in Turkey. Whoops! The lesson I learned here was: **that if** someone has fifty mission crushes in their hats, try to think of an alternative to jail.

ERHAC TURKEY: GENERAL GOKERI

Erhac Turkey, Security Police, 1st LT Chris Peterson - 150 miles south of Russia

After two-and-a-half years in the air force, I was on my way to a Turkish air base in Erhac, Turkey. The American mission there was to protect and arm weapons that would fly North to Russia if necessary. We were in Eastern Turkey about one-hundred-and-fifty miles South of the Russian border. There were only eighty Americans on the base, about

30

twenty-five of which were airmen working for me in the security police unit.

For the most part, my job was security-related and not so much law enforcement. The base commander was a Turkish General, Gokerii, who was a fighter pilot. For some strange reason, General Gokerii took a liking to me. I had been promoted to captain by this time, but it was still a bit awkward to be regularly invited to have chai tea with the general.

A memorable incident on the base involved one of my sergeants who reported he had been robbed of his cigarettes at gunpoint while on patrol. The suspect was a Turk security person. American cigarettes were obviously popular with the Turks. I was scheduled to have chai with the general that morning, and during my tea time, I mentioned the robbery to him.

LT. COL. RAY GERFEN

Later that day, a very annoyed Lt. Col. Ray Gerfen accosted me. He was my boss, the commanding officer of all the American airmen on the base, and I had forgotten to report to him about the robbery. He had gone to see General Gokerii that morning, and there was blood all over his office. The general explained to Lt. Col. Gerfen that he had personally beat the offending Turk. Gerfen cooled off after a couple of days. We remained friends for the rest of Ray Gerfen's life.

My active-duty time ended after a year in Turkey. During that tenure, I applied for jobs in law enforcement and related fields. One application was to the Multnomah County Sheriff's Office (M.C.S.O.) in Portland, OR. This agency was one of the first local law enforcement agencies that required a four-year college degree. My application was accepted, and an arduous process that included written, physical, and psychological testing ensued.

PART II

Chapter 4

M.C.S.O. APPLICATION PROCESS 1971

As a captain in the air force, I could be choosy about picking an employer. My pay grade then was much higher than any entry-level law enforcement job I might get. Multnomah County was top on my list for a couple of reasons. First, I fell in love with Portland while I was in the area as a college freshman. Second, the recruitment presentation by Don Clark back in my college days made it seem very appealing.

The Multnomah County Sheriff's Office had about two-hundred-and-thirty sworn officers, while the Portland Police Department had about three times that many. The sheriff's office patrolled the unincorporated area of the county and had some broad countywide duties such as river patrol and narcotics. The sheriff's office also ran the county jail system, and those officers were classified as "corrections officers." Geographically the patrol area of the county was comparable in size, but the city was more heavily populated than the unincorporated areas.

One of the funnier moments during the application process was the psych testing. I was impressed by the shrink who administered the evaluation. He asked all kinds of offensive questions about my mother and other strange inquiries. One of his last evaluations was to show me ten ink blots called a Rorschach Test. He asked me what I saw in the ink blots. On the first one, I said, "It looks like a bunch of rats eating each other." I gave that same answer nine more times. I assumed that would eliminate me from the process, but I didn't care at that point in time. If a shrink is ever bothering you, just talk about rats. It worked for me! I was

Multnomah County Sheriff Patch and history of the organization

hired as a Multnomah County Deputy in Portland, OR in June of 1971.

This was an exciting time for me. It started out a bit slow, as we could not carry a gun or do anything significant until we went through the police academy. For several months I worked in the radio room, rode around with guys serving arrest warrants, and did a lot of other boring busywork. One of the guys I served warrants with named Vern, was at the end of his career; thus, we were always in low gear. He served many warrants on inmates in the county jail and would arrange his visits to coincide with lunchtime. We would eat in the jail with food prepared by inmates. All I can say is "Yuk," but nevertheless, I loved you, Vern.

METRO POLICE ACADEMY FOR P.P.D. & M.C.S.O. CANDIDATES

In September of 1971, I was finally in a real police academy. This was a Metro Police Academy, so three-quarters of the cadets were from the Portland Police Department, and the remainder were cadets from the M.C.S.O. Being unfamiliar with Portland and knowing virtually no one in the area, the academy was a great experience. I made lifelong friends with many Portland officers, which served me well over the course of my career. In a few months, I would find myself working in a patrol district that adjoined the Portland Police jurisdiction. At the academy, we were seated alphabetically. In my row, there were Owens, Pahlke, Peterson, Perry, and Powell. Of these, only two retired after a full career. Steve Owens died in a line of duty death early in his career, and Kent Perry was shot by a high-powered rifle while working. Fortunately,

Kent had a long and successful career as a detective despite his injuries.

The academy was twelve weeks long, and it was held in a large windowless bomb shelter at Kelly Butte in SE Portland. This structure had been constructed as a location for the city government to flee in the event of a catastrophe. The training was certainly well done and adequate for the next step in our police careers. We were then assigned to a Field Training Officer (F.T.O.). The F.T.O.'s all had several years of experience. At this time in 1971, the department was now hiring only college graduates. It often felt as if there was a subtle undercurrent of animosity among some of the coaches towards the college boys.

Chris Peterson Academy Graduation

Multnomah County Sheriff Office ID - signed by Don Clark.

NEW CATHAY & JOHNNY CHIN

A nearby restaurant in my district was The New Cathay, which was located on the corner of 82nd and SE Division St. in Portland. I quickly learned that this was a favorite stop for police officers and cadets. The New Cathay charged the police half price for meals. There were a number of restaurants in Portland that treated the police similarly. The practice of free meals was strictly forbidden by the sheriff's office. Keeping this rule in mind, when I got a bill for half price, I would leave a tip to cover the full bill. I was comfortable with still paying the bill amount, and the waitresses enjoyed the tips.

This practice was understandable on the part of the owners, as they liked the police presence, particularly in the tougher parts of town. One of the owners of the New Cathay was John Chin, who was of Chinese ancestry. He was a WWII vet and genuinely liked cops. Many of the cops that worked in SE Portland grew to love John, and it wasn't just for the cheap food. I got to know many of the patrons and counted them as friends. Every night the eating counter of the New Cathay would fill up with retired folks. In many respects, it became their living room, a home away from home. At Christmas time every year, John would put up a caricature of a Chinese Santa, and underneath it read "Melly Clismus." I was a regular in the New Cathay all of my police career.

Chapter 5

UNIFORM/ FOUR MONTHS WITH COACHES: 1972-1974

Normally, we would be with a coach or Field Training Officer (F.T.O.) for a month before moving on to another. As we rotated through them, it was expected that we would start to handle calls without a lot of input. This was tough for the coaches, as they could see things getting out of hand at times but had to let rookies wade through each call by themselves. After three or four months, I got to go out on my own, even though I still had a lot to learn.

ON MY OWN: FIRST DRUNK

One of my first unpleasant encounters occurred at night while on patrol. I saw a drunk driver, turned on the B-rays or blue lights, and pulled him over. Unfamiliar with the county, I was not exactly sure where I was but soon found myself fighting with an ironworker who was more than a handful. As the battle went on, I maintained but was running out of steam. I finally had a chance to get on the radio and called for cover. Of course, the first thing the dispatcher asked was, "Where are you?" I didn't know; I couldn't see any street signs. I remembered seeing tall billboards overhead, so I told the dispatcher that I could see a 7-Up billboard.

Unfortunately, that wasn't particularly helpful. Coaches had likely told me several times to know where you are when you make a traffic stop. My real education started that night in East Multnomah County.

COUNTY TOPOGRAPHY

Unincorporated Multnomah County was very diverse. On the East end of the county, there was a stretch known as the Columbia Gorge, which is one of the most beautiful places in the world. This area consists of high basalt cliffs, numerous waterfalls, and the Columbia River separating the state of Oregon from Washington. On the other side of the county were the West Hills, where the rich people lived. There was also Sauvie Island which was a bucolic twenty-mile-long island in the Columbia River with rich farmland and beaches. The center of the unincorporated county was diverse as well. There were a number of nice areas mixed in with pockets of poverty and crime. My career started in these shadowy pockets. I got to work briefly on the West side of the county as I started my career. The West Hills were tough to find your way around, being hilly with very few through streets. While patrolling those areas, I was always lost.

SALEM KIDNAP/ ROBBERY

During One of those early night shifts on the West side, I decided to stop at the airport to visit some Port of Portland

Police Officers. The West side was generally pretty quiet, but the airport was a long way from where I was technically supposed to be. I was happily visiting with my new friends when an urgent dispatch came over the radio. There was a robbery and kidnapping in Salem, fifty miles South of Portland. Normally that would not get much attention in Portland, but the suspects were now headed north on I-5 towards our city with two victims in their car. There were probably fifteen police cars following the suspects, and they were headed toward my district. Traffic was quiet, but I was also about ten miles from my assigned district. I headed West with lights and sirens on, what police call "Code 3." As I got within a couple of miles of the activity, a Portland Police Officer got in behind me, headed for the same call. I was glad to have company, but I was really lost. Miracles do happen, and quite by accident, I made it to the traffic stop involving the kidnappers.

When I arrived at the scene, there were twelve to fifteen police cars surrounding the bad guys, completely circling the offenders. All the officers had guns out and pointed toward the car. One of the suspects was out of the car at gunpoint, crawling like a snake. It occurred to me that if someone had farted loudly, it could have caused everyone to start shooting. On my first call to a felony traffic stop, I backed about a quarter of a mile up a nearby hill and watched from that distance. The lesson I learned here was: if you ever find

43

yourself completely surrounded by guns, move very slowly away and remain quiet.

MY BEAT: ERROL HEIGHTS/ FELONY FLATS/ THE SQUIRREL

My first real assignment wasn't on the West side of the Columbia River Gorge; it was Errol Heights, affectionately known by us cops as "Felony Flats" or "Squirrel Heights." This was a SE Portland area where a large number of the residents had been in the "State Pen" or incarcerated elsewhere several times. A lot of the streets were not paved and did not receive routine maintenance. The district was bad enough that the sheriff's office had decided to make it their only two-man car area in the department, so we all rode with a partner.

I spent about a year working at Errol Heights and had two great partners during this time: Garry Christensen and Jerry Hill. We had all been hired at about the same time and were excited to be working in this district. Both of these guys had played football in college, so they were physically up to the task. More importantly, they were genuinely excited to be working as cops in such a high-crime area.

LEARNING SURVIVAL SKILLS

Working at Errol Heights was probably the best assignment I could have had as a rookie police officer. There was no more theory, no more coaching, and you ran into folks every day who would be happy to kill you should the need arise. It was here that we started learning real survival skills. We discovered what the "dope fiends" we had studied in college were really all about. Speed and heroin were the drugs of choice in the Heights. Burglaries were rampant, and the good citizens in the area were basically prisoners in their own homes.

BURGLARS

One of the most poignant memories of my early career involved a modest eight-hundred-square-foot house where an elderly man and his wife lived. He was a blue-collar worker who had toiled his whole life and was now retired. He had purchased a twelve-foot aluminum boat and was getting ready to relax and start fishing. Unfortunately, the burglars in the area terrorized this house. His home was burglarized several times, and he finally created an elaborate alarm system that amounted to a bunch of aluminum cans tied to a fishing line. The fishing line was hard to see, and burglars would trip over it, causing the cans to fall. The clatter of the cans was his way of fishing and the primary alarm system at the residence. With a great deal of satisfaction, one of my first felony arrests was a juvenile burglar at his house. In spite of my best efforts, the man never really got to spend much time fishing, as he was afraid to leave his wife's home alone. Now I was getting an insider's view of crime and how it impacted good folks.

OUTLAW BIKERS

I remember a call about unwanted "Bikers" at the Checkered Flag Tavern in Errol Heights. Dispatch was trying to find me a cover car, someone to give me backup, but I told them that I would advise if I needed assistance. I knew a lot of the bikers, including the president of the local club Darwin Hicks. I walked into the tavern, and sure enough, there were a bunch of bikers, including Darwin. I walked up to him with a smile on my face and told him that they needed to leave due to the owner's complaints. Darwin was pleasant and said they would all leave. This seemed just a bit too easy, though, so I told Darwin that I would have to arrest him if they came back.

Of course, a couple of hours later, they were back, and I got the call to return. I went in calmly, walked up to Darwin, handcuffed him, and took him to jail. Darwin Hicks could have been a handful if he wanted to be. He had been in prison and was all pumped up from lifting weights while incarcerated. Darwin left willingly with me, and much to my surprise, he actually showed up for court a few months later.

In Judge Kim Frankel's Multnomah County courtroom, the first thing I saw that day was Darwin, all muscled up, wearing a black t-shirt with the inscription "Blame it on the Bikers." I had to chuckle and tell him that the t-shirt may not have been a good idea. I do not think Darwin and I ever had crosswords; we understood each other.

SHOOTING AT THE HORSE AND COW

Another tavern in Errol Heights was the Horse and Cow. It was apparently a required stop for recently released prison inmates. Many of us young, hard-charging cops would make regular stops at the place and others like it. We quickly got to know who the local bad guys were, what cars they drove, and who they hung out with. We made a lot of warrant arrests involving this tavern.

I called in sick one night, and my partner Jerry Hill had a replacement for the shift. They made a stop at the Horse and Cow, and Jerry walked up to the bar. Jerry's partner was standing close when a con at the bar swiveled and stuck a gun in Jerry's stomach. The con had apparently not noticed a third cop, Tom Anderson, known lovingly as "T-Bone," some distance away from Jerry and his replacement partner. "T-Bone" shot and killed the con who had a gun in Jerry's stomach. Another Lesson I learned that day was: that calling in sick can sometimes be a good idea.

STOLEN SILVER

Another early case I was assigned was the arrest of a burglar who had invaded an elderly lady's house. One of the items stolen was the woman's beloved silverware set. The price of silver had gone sky high, up to $50 an ounce, and real silverware became a hot item for the local burglars. Many years later, I can still see the wonderful smile on the lady's face as she got her silverware back. This is one of the joys that cops have in life when they are given the opportunity to do their jobs.

ELDERLY MURDER

Early in my career, while working in the Heights, an elderly woman was murdered by a burglar. Although I wasn't involved in the case, I went to the courthouse to watch part of the murder trial and sat immediately behind the defense table. The defense attorney was Mark Blackman. While he was making his impassioned plea, I observed the killer reach over and jerk on his coattails. He pointed at the clock; it was a few minutes past noon. He then casually asked, "Is it time for lunch?" Having been on the stand opposite these lawyers before, this was one of the few times I ever felt sorry for a criminal defense attorney.

CIGARETTE THIEF

One night Jerry and I saw a beater of a car going down the street with a trail of sparks shooting out from behind where the muffler was dragging on the road. We were in the area of the Horse and Cow on SE Foster Rd. It was enough to get our attention, and we pulled the car over, only to discover that the driver was drunk. We also found dozens of cartons of cigarettes in the back seat. After some superb detective work, we determined that the cigarettes were stolen.

As we were sitting in our prowl car with the blue overhead lights going, the Multnomah County Sheriff's logo was clearly visible on the side. We had the driver in the back seat and processed the arrest by getting a tow truck to our location. Just then, a doper came wandering down the sidewalk, looked into the car at all of the stolen cigarettes, and began to remove several cartons while we were sitting there watching. As he started to leave, we got out, arrested him for stealing the stolen cigarettes, and hauled the two fools off to jail together in the back seat.

STUTTERING BOB

Both of my partners, Garry and Jerry, were highly motivated, and a night without a felony arrest was time wasted for us. One night Jerry and I stopped a well know outlaw biker. Let's just call him "Stuttering Bob" to protect the guilty. Among a host of crimes, we discovered that Bob was a felon in possession of a handgun, and then we kept finding charges to add to the growing list. Needless to say, Bob was escorted to jail, and we felt good about taking another local criminal off the streets.

JENNY HILL LABOR

While we were dealing with Stuttering Bob, county records started calling us on the radio. They wanted Jerry to call home, but he was too busy to make the call. As the pleas for him to call home grew more frantic, I got involved. Jerry's wife was going into labor with their daughter. I drove to his house and made him get into the back seat. I put Jenny in the front seat with me, and we made the hospital run. Several hours later, Christa was born. All these years later, I am still in touch with Christa on her birthday.

NEW CATHAY BAR

The bar that was a part of the New Cathay Restaurant poured generous drinks. One night I was seated in the restaurant eating by myself when three unruly drunks walked out of the adjoining bar, passing within ten feet of me as they headed for the exit. John was standing near the door and cash register. He told the drunks that they had not paid for their meals. They started obnoxiously running their mouths. I watched for a few minutes and then got up to explain the facts of life to them. I do not think they saw me sitting there in uniform, but they weren't too concerned when I made my presence known. Finally, one of them pulled the bill out and paid it. As they left, another one of them turned and kicked the glass door so hard that I thought it would shatter. I went out and grabbed the asshole, but as I looked over my shoulder, one of his sidekicks was starting to swing at my back.

I was focused on the three drunks and had my hands full when a wonderful voice came out of nowhere and said, "Go ahead and hit the officer. I am an old man with nothing to lose." There was my friend John, a seventy-year-old, with a shiny meat cleaver in his hand. John and his wife became friends, and we had a wonderful relationship socializing for years.

WALLY

One night, I was dispatched to a house near 148th and East Burnside St. It was a family beef call, otherwise known as a domestic disturbance. As I walked up to the front porch, I could see that it was supported by two 4x4 posts, but one of them was shattered. That should have been a clue as to how events would unfold. I went into the house and saw a man named Wally spread out casually in an easy chair. I tried to talk with him, but my communication was not going well. Looking out the window, I saw several of my friends watching to see how good my negotiating skills were. One of the memorable faces was Sgt. Harold Swank. Harold was a big, bald man with a partial dental plate. When he thought there was going to be a fight, he took the partial out, exposing his missing front tooth. When I saw Harold's tooth missing, I gulped because he had way more experience than I did. Sure enough, my negotiating skills were weak, and the fight was on. Three to four more guys came in, and we managed to get Wally under control with a lot of effort.

Off to the hospital, we went, and Wally got a shot of Thorazine. One shot was normally sufficient to quiet folks down, but not for Wally, so he got a second shot. Although he became a bit calmer, the E.R. doc decided that he needed to go to the nearby mental hospital. So off we went in an ambulance with Wally handcuffed and tied to a gurney. The shrink came out to speak with me; he was about five-foot-two inches tall with a big mouth. He saw Wally trussed up like a Christmas goose and said, "Why do you cops always overreact to these people?" I won't tell you what I told Wally about the shrink as we quietly untrussed him and left him in the good doctor's care.

About two years into the job, I was rotated to detectives. I was very happy working patrol at night, and I told my boss,

52

Lt. R.W. Miller, that I didn't want to leave patrol; I was having fun. I enjoyed working for R.W., and he told me that I shouldn't question it. Looking back, he was correct. It was a good decision overall and formed the basis for the rest of my career. Lt. Miller's suggestion was the shove that I needed. Little did I know at the time that there was a big, interesting career ahead of me.

Chapter 6

DETECTIVES: 1975-1977

One of my partners from my uniform days was Garry Christensen. We understood each other and always anticipated what the other person would do. We transitioned easily into detective work together, as he was my partner again in this new assignment. We were placed in the Property Crimes section. In our case, we were immediately working on burglaries. This also translated into narcotic's work, as most of the criminals were using drugs and committing crimes to support their habit. The more experienced officers were generally working the Person Crimes section, which included crimes like robbery and murder.

LEGENDARY BLACKIE YAZZOLINO

There was a legendary Multnomah County detective working Person Crimes. His name was Orlando "Blackie" Yazzolino. Blackie had worked homicide for years. We young guys didn't wander into Blackie's office often. He was sort of a mythical figure, as he didn't leave his desk a lot. Blackie grew up in Portland and was from an Italian family that was significant in the law enforcement community and the city at large. He knew his way around and could accomplish a lot from his desk. In the 1970s, Blackie was named Police Officer of the Month in a national publication called *Master Detective*. Like Peter Falk's well-known persona, he became the "Columbo" of the Northwest among his peers. He started his career with the Portland Police Department in 1941 and moved to Multnomah County in 1961. His prolific career spanned thirty-one years.

OFF AND RUNNING: LEARNING THE ROPES

I remember my first detective case. Someone had snatched a six-pack of Budweiser from a market, and a witness got the license plate of the suspect's car and the type of beer that had been stolen. This petty crime rose to the level of robbery, as some force had been used by the suspect. I found the perpetrator's house, looked into the kitchen window, and saw the beer sitting in the cupboard. After obtaining a search warrant for the house, I subsequently arrested the thief. There must have been some guffaws and snide comments about my first big case, but I didn't care. Now I was off and running.

BURGLARY T.A.C. UNIT: ENGLERT/ WOODS & CHRISTENSEN/ PETERSON

Garry Christensen and I worked closely with partners Joe Woods and Rod Englert during this time. They were older and more experienced than we were, but nevertheless, there was a constant competition to see which team would make the first felony arrest every day. Joe and Rod went on to work homicide together years later. They became well-known and highly respected in that arena. In retirement, Rod became a world-renowned blood splatter expert and crime scene reconstructionist, consulting on cases all over the U.S. I am proud to call him a friend, and through my private investigation company, we continue to work on homicide cases together.

The four of us had a lot of fun during these days, and our stories were varied, to say the least. One time we learned about a serious felon that had a warrant and was reporting monthly to his parole officer. In collaboration with the P.O., we waited for our suspect to show up. As he went into his appointment, Rod got into the back of the guy's van and waited. When the man came back out and entered his vehicle, Rod put a gun on his back and told him that the police were visiting him. Talk about scaring the shit out of someone.

Another time we went to a suspect's apartment to arrest him for a robbery. Joe's gun was holstered on his belt. Once inside the apartment, Joe pulled the gun to point at the bad guy, and his holster came out with it. As we looked towards Joe, we saw him pointing his holstered gun toward the man.

This is just one of the funny moments in police life where things ended right rather than the alternative.

Years later, Joe and Rod were investigating a murder. The victim had been beaten to death in his Portland accounting office with a pool ball in a sock. A year after the murder, Joe, and Rod had a diver search the Columbia River near the suspected murder weapon dump site along Marine Drive. Keep in mind that this is a big river, a mile wide, in this location. The sock and pool ball were recovered and aided in the conviction of the suspect. The Lesson here is: good investigators dig in improbable spots.

ASTORIA, OR

Early in my detective career, a burglary tactical and undercover unit was created. About this time, Garry and I were working with two other detectives who had similar levels of experience. For about two years, the unit averaged arresting four to five burglars a week. There were a lot of good stories during this time period. One of my first moves in this undercover role was to change my appearance in order to fit into the criminal underworld, so I grew facial hair and a big afro. We were also assigned a variety of undercover vehicles that all looked like junkers.

During one operation, Garry and I were driving a yellow Ford Econoline van that looked like a dirtbag vehicle. One day, an acquaintance told me of his plans to commit two burglaries on the coast. He wanted to know if I would haul him and his friends to Astoria, OR. I agreed, and the next day we were headed to the beach with the bad guys in the back of the van doing dope. Little did they know, we had called ahead and notified the local police in Astoria of our situation, creating a plan for them to stop us without blowing our cover.

The suspects committed two burglaries while we waited. The arranged plan with the police was for me to hit my brakes three times when we were ready for the traffic stop to be made on us. I tapped my brakes lightly a couple of times, but no one stopped us. I then told the suspects I was going inside a local store to get some beer. An undercover officer met me inside the store, and I asked if they didn't stop us. It turned out that the van brake lights weren't working. This is just one example of how important the ability to improvise is when a plan goes astray.

The stop eventually got made, and the good guys managed to escape without their covers being blown. The bad guys got arrested. Their court-appointed attorney told the local detectives his clients were just hitchhiking and did not know anything about the stolen property in the van. The local detective asked if the attorney had looked at the police reports yet, and he said that he had not. This detective suggested that the attorney sits on that story until he saw the report describing the undercover operation and planned traffic stop. Of course, once the story was known, the burglars all pled guilty.

FIVE BURGLARS

That yellow Ford Econoline van brings back a lot of memories. One day we had five young burglars in the back of it with enough evidence to arrest them all. The van had curtains all the way around. Garry and I drove to our office at 2nd and SE Oak St. in the heart of downtown Portland with the five burglars still sitting in the van. They had no idea that we were going to arrest them. We pulled up in front of the office and sprung the surprise on the burglars. None of them had a clue where we were due to the curtains all the way around except for the windshield. With all five handcuffed and trailing behind us, we looked like a mother duck walking our ducklings into the building.

FAMOUS AUTO THIEF

M.C.S.O. had three detectives who were world-class auto theft investigators: Walt Hawkins, Jerry Baumgartner, and Noble Keist. Sometimes these iconic detectives would ask us to assist them. One such occasion involved a prolific auto thief named Sonny B., who was very active in the general Portland area at the time. His specialty seemed to be four-wheel drive pickups.

One day Garry and I were on Hwy. 30 in Jerry Baumgartner's detective car. We were headed East into Portland when Jerry saw two pickups headed West. Jerry thought that it was Sonny B. in the first pickup. There was another four-wheel drive vehicle behind the first pickup. Jerry did an immediate u-turn, and we were now following the two pickups as they drove West from Portland. Jerry made the correct assumption that the second pickup was stolen. Both trucks exited the highway and headed into an area known as Forest Park in NW Portland. The two drivers quickly realized that they were being followed, and the chase was now on. We activated the siren and grill lights on our undercover car. Sonny B. noticed Garry waving a gun out the window, so he finally decided to stop.

Garry got out to arrest Sonny, and we left him alone with Sonny standing by his pickup. Jerry and I were now chasing the stolen truck at high speeds on a gravel road in a hilly area. We decided the best way to de-escalate the situation was to shoot out a tire. Since Jerry was driving, I was the one tasked with attempting the impossible. I started aiming at the right rear tire and fired three or four shots at the fast-moving target on this windy gravel road. After a short distance, the pickup ran off of the road over a steep embankment. The driver got out and escaped into a forested area. We ultimately got the truck out of the brush. What we didn't know at the time was that a third thief was lying in the bed of the pickup and had been unscrewing the bolts that attached the canopy, making it ready to remove. Unbeknownst to us at the time, that third thief had escaped as well.

After this encounter, the auto theft guys started doing their magic. They determined the identity of both the driver and the thief who was in the bed of the truck. They also located a forested area nearby where the stolen vehicles were being stripped. There was a lot of evidence found at this location, including some spent shotgun shells. These shotgun shells became useful pieces of evidence. A search warrant was subsequently carried out on Sonny's house, which was miles away, and those spent shells were linked forensically to a shotgun in his house. There were a number of other charges that arose out of this event.

One tidbit that I still enjoy today came from the owner of the stolen pickup. He got his vehicle back in pretty good condition, and it only required some minor work. The insurance company asked if he wanted the rear bumper replaced, as there were three small dimples in the heavy steel above the right rear tire. The owner of the pickup was proud of the three dimples my two-inch .38 revolver had put in his bumper during the chase. He said, "Hell no, I don't want the bumper replaced, and I hope the next asshole who decides to steal my truck realizes what caused those dimples." I never was a great shot in all my years of carrying guns as a soldier and law enforcement officer. This one day in my long career, I was pretty good, though. Shooting at a fast-moving vehicle that was sliding on a gravel road trying to outrun us, I hit the bumper three times above the right rear tire. It may not have been a complete success since I didn't hit the tire, but I also did not hit the thief in the bed of the truck. The Lesson learned here is some days, you just get lucky.

KEPPLER: ARMED ROBBER/ MURDERER

Billie Keppler was an interesting guy from New York. We got to know Billie after arresting him. His parents were upstanding citizens, and Billie had an opportunity to play professional football until he was injured and let go from the team. He got involved with painkillers after this injury and subsequently turned to heroin in a big way. He would occasionally come into the office and visit with us. The experienced detectives did not like him around. One day, a teletype came through describing a robbery suspect. The description fit Billie, and there was little doubt who it was. Like that, the search was on.

Garry and I knew Billie went to the Henry Building in downtown Portland to get his methadone early every morning. We staked the methadone clinic out waiting for Billie to get his dose, and when he came out of the building, we arrested him. Billie had been in prison recently, and he was all bulked up from pumping iron in the joint. We had to be quick apprehending him, as there were a dozen or more junkies standing around. They all became belligerent and aggressive. To them, the Henry Building was a safe haven, and it was being invaded.

We handcuffed Billie and walked him to our office two blocks away. When we got into the elevator, he said, "Garry and Chris, I like you guys. I have a gun hidden in the small of my back."

Sure enough, Billie was right. Not properly searching a suspect is one of the mistakes that officers sometimes make, particularly young ones. Those kinds of mistakes can be fatal. We did not charge Billie for the gun possession charge, and he pled guilty to the robberies. The day that we arrested Billie, he was wearing a leather vest that had the quintessential bad guy look to it. Before Billie went to prison, he passed that vest on to me. He gave it to me as a friend, and I wore it for some time as an undercover cop. Sadly, after getting out of jail years later, Billie was involved in a robbery where someone was killed, and he went back to prison for a long time.

JUVENILE BURGLARS

Working burglary cases in the 70s was a bit like working dope because most of the burglars were dopers as well. We learned a lot about narcotics during this period of time, even though we were not assigned to a dope unit. Marijuana was not legal anywhere back in those days. A high percentage of the juvenile burglars that we arrested were daily users. They had lost all ambition and would steal a stereo or T.V. to sell in order to buy some dope to get high. We became proficient at getting statements from all of these burglars. I would sit them down to write out a statement, telling me how they got into the house, what they took, etc. The statements all had a similarity to them. These criminals would ring the doorbell first to see if anyone was home and then find an out-of-sight place to break in. They would then take a pillowcase to carry out the loot. I let them make errors in spelling and grammar because I did not want to make the statements look like I wrote them.

Once, while talking to a senior district attorney (D.A.) about a burglary case, he said, "I'll get your ass one day." I was a bit surprised at his attitude and asked what he was talking about. He said that he knew how I was getting all the signed confessions and insinuated that I was beating the shit out of the suspects. I was totally enraged and slammed his office door so hard when I left that it shook the wall. The D.A. was totally wrong, but in fairness to him, no one in his office had ever seen the kind of production we were doing.

One of the interesting side notes to this story is that cops are constantly challenged by defense attorneys, particularly on the witness stand. There is a training program called The Reid Techniques of Interviewing. It espouses a particular way of conducting interviews. Attorneys would routinely ask me on the witness stand if I had attended this training. They were hoping to show that I had coerced confessions. I never had any training in regard to statement-taking or obtaining confessions. I had a lot of training about the legal aspects of statements and interviews. The legal system and criminal defense establishment relish going after cops and their statement-taking ability. A lot of us were just good at it. I hear all kinds of stories about all the so-called experts who get confessions and statements. Local detectives are probably the best in the world at this because it is almost a daily activity and often involves the most serious crimes.

CROOKED COPS

One day, an informant contacted Garry Christensen and me to tell us that a female known as Carol M. would be waiting for her boyfriend Stanley as he walked out of a courtroom after being sentenced for armed robbery. The informant had been told that Carol would pass a balloon of heroin to Stanley when she kissed him in the hallway. We did not know what Carol looked like, and there were a number of people in the hallway of the courthouse when we arrived there in plain clothes, undercover. As we cautiously surveyed the crowd, the kiss took place, but we did not intercept the heroin.

We introduced ourselves to Carol, and she took us to her house. She showed us where she was storing stolen property in her basement and told us about the burglaries she was involved with. We left her house and went back to our office, asking each other, "Did you hear what I heard?" After discussing the situation, we went to Carol's house, arrested her for the burglaries, and brought her to the office to make a statement.

We did not have a lot of female officers in the department in the mid-'70s, so we asked a secretary to assist us in patting down Carol. In the process, our secretary Maggie was assaulted. It wasn't a serious assault, but it was still irritating, to say the least. We put Carol in our undercover car and headed toward the county jail. This undercover vehicle did not have a "cage" in the backseat, and Carol was manhandled in the process of trying to escape custody. She ultimately sued the department for her alleged mistreatment and was successfully awarded some money. This incident did not go over well with our superiors, to say the least.

EXILED TO RADIO DISPATCH

Captain Harold Amidon decided that Garry and I had made a mistake in the Carol issue and chose to punish us. We were told that one of us was going to be transferred to radio dispatch. This move was a huge demotion from uniform patrol and detective work. When we asked which one of us it was going to be, he told us to make our own decision. Garry and I flipped a coin, and I lost. Just like that, away I went to that place where real cops did not want to go: the monotony of desk duty at radio dispatch. I spent a year working the radio on the swing shift, and I learned a lot about the communications system. I also made a lot of friends while doing my time. One evening while I was being punished at the radio desk, we had a tense situation, and I was able to talk some guy into surrendering while on the phone with him. Lt. Jim Dillard, who was in charge of swing shift patrol at the time, put me in for an "Attaboy." An "Attaboy" is a citation that I received in this case for talking the person out of a very bad decision. The Lesson I learned here was: you just can't keep a good man down.

After Carol was in jail, I got contacted by a Portland narcotics detective named Bill. He said Carol was working for him and that he did not want her arrested. He went on to say that he would testify for her in court. We did not believe him, and sadly enough, a short time later, we discovered that there were a number of rogue dope cops in the Portland narcotics unit. They had been making a lot of bogus arrests and planting dope during search warrants. The case that brought this matter to light was a dope case at an outlaw biker club in North Portland. The Portland Dope Unit was serving a warrant on the location, and a Portland narcotics detective was shot and killed while attempting to enter the building.

This incident had a lot of ironies, but one of those was the fact that the defense attorney who represented one of the bikers was Des Connell. Until shortly before this incident, Des had been the elected Multnomah County District Attorney. He went on to a long, successful career as a Portland criminal defense attorney. During the investigation of this shooting, it became clear that there was going to be dope planted by the Portland undercover cops at the biker location. The Portland Police officer who was killed in the raid had dope in his pocket before entry was made into the house. This incident was a terrible blemish on the Portland dope cops, and it confirmed what I had thought about several of them all along.

KIM MURPHY

Garry Christensen and I arrested a burglar named Kim Murphy for a commercial burglary of an electronics business. We learned a lot from Kim, as he shared his modus operandi (M.O.) with us during the interrogation. At his arraignment, he told the judge that he needed to be released from custody so that he could raise some money to aid in his defense. The next day Mr. Murphy was "raising money for his defense" by robbing a liquor store in SE Portland. A Portland police officer, John Folliard, pursued Murphy into Creston Park after the robbery. Murphy shot and wounded him. I am always amused by the progressive folks who feel that non-violent crimes like narcotic violations and property crimes such as theft and burglary should be dealt with lightly.

COUNTERFEITERS

A highlight of my early career was an episode in the mid-70s. The tactical burglary unit got involved in buying some stolen property from a few well-known burglars. Prior to meeting with them and exchanging money for the stolen property, the crooks told us they needed a female to cash in some stolen money orders. We had a shortage of female officers at the time, so I recruited my wife Diana to assist us. I know this sounds like a terrible idea, and I must admit to having been stupid more than once. Diana did a great job of playacting, and the crooks were happy to have her assist in their endeavor.

Diana, another undercover officer, named Tom Seibert, and I were in the crooks' house. They wanted to use a typewriter to put names on the stolen money orders. Their typewriter wasn't functioning, so Tom came to the rescue and fixed it. He had learned that trade in the army. The plan was for Diana to pass the stolen money orders to the crooks. She had been instructed to go out the front door at the appropriate time, signal to the group of officers hiding outside, and have them come in to assist with the arrests.

As Diana went outside, I pulled my gun and badge out. The crooks were so preoccupied with the fact that they would soon be cashing all of their stolen money orders that they didn't immediately realize their scheme had suddenly come un-glued. One of them was carrying a hidden handgun. There were three to five people arrested without incident. Consequently, Garry and I had to write a lot of reports.

KEN PHILLIPS ARREST: L.A.P.D.

We were in our office writing reports until late in the evening when the phone rang. It was the county jail telling us that an inmate wanted to talk to a detective. When we asked what he wanted to talk about, the corrections officers didn't have any idea. We were the only county detectives around, so I called my boss Capt. Amidon at home. He asked what the inmate wanted, and I told him that I had no idea. Amidon's response was, "Go ahead, but make it quick." He was trying to save on overtime, of course.

The inmate's name was Ken Phillips, and we learned that he was in custody for breaking into a vacant house to sleep. This would likely have been charged as a misdemeanor trespass case; it was not a big issue. We introduced ourselves to Phillips and quickly learned that he was literally a farm boy from Utah with no significant record. He asked us, "Where do you want me to start?" We were a bit puzzled by the question but soon realized that he thought he had been caught at something significant. Although neither of us had a clue what it was, we played along to see where this story might lead. After a bit of psych gymnastics, I said, "Why don't you start with the last one." My mind was really going nuts, not knowing what would come out of his mouth.

Phillips told us that just before he got arrested, he had robbed Nendels in Beaverton at gunpoint. Nendels was a restaurant and motel fifteen miles from where he was arrested. He said the monkey mask, the gun, and the $500 taken in the robbery were hidden in the crawl space of the house where he was arrested. We took him to the house and recovered the items right where he said they would be.

The significant issue that came out of the Phillips arrest was the clearing of nearly a dozen armed robberies in Los Angeles, CA. A clearance means that he gave us enough information about each case that he could most likely be charged successfully with those crimes. It was difficult to write this type of report as one didn't have dates, addresses, victims' names, or possibly even the name of the establishment he had robbed. He was subsequently convicted of robbery in Los Angeles. We did our best to get what was needed for the charges in L.A. We sent the reports to L.A.P.D., and they ended up in the Robbery-Homicide Division (R.H.D.) unit. The widely held belief about L.A.P.D.'s R.H.D. unit is that they are one of the more elite detective squads within the Los Angeles Police Department.

This case was a good example of being quick on your feet when doing interviews. You never know what will come out of interrogation. One of my usual last questions was always, "Is there something else we should talk about?" I have gotten several interesting answers to that question over the years.

Chapter 7

MY FRIENDS AT LAPD

Our reports on Phillips ended up on the desk of Det. Sgt. Jack A. Giroud. Jack was assigned to the motel robbery section. He only had about twenty years on the job at the time, so he was "still learning." Jack had started with L.A.P.D. in 1956. Twenty years after Jack was hired, I had the privilege of meeting him. He was one of the giants in West Coast law enforcement. Jack was six-foot-three inches tall, weighed three-hundred-plus pounds, and had a booming voice that matched his physical description. Keep in mind that Garry and I were still really rookies at this point in time and had only been on the job for about four years.

After Jack read our reports, he contacted us and said, "The D.A.'s office in L.A. wants me to come and get statements from Phillips, so they don't have to bring you guys to California for arraignment and a possible trial." Jack asked if we were interested in going to L.A. for court, and of course, we said, "Hell yes!" It was raining in Oregon. Jack and his partner Lou McClary flew to Oregon, and we took them to the state pen where Phillips was housed.

Let me remind you once again that Sgt. Det. Jack Giroud was a big guy with a booming voice. When we got inside the prison, Jack said to the prisoner, "I am Detective Jack Giroud. You do not want to talk to me, do you boy?" Phillips said, "No, sir. I guess not." Jack turned to me and said, "I told those people at the D.A.'s office that he wouldn't talk to me."

Shortly thereafter, Garry and I were headed to L.A. for the arraignment of Phillips, even though the same process in Oregon would have taken all of fifteen minutes. On our first night there, Jack arranged for his wife to drive us around L.A. As sworn peace officers, we respect the laws of drinking and driving but having a sober chauffeur allowed us all to apply adult beverages liberally. The next day, I was on the witness stand for five hours with a world-class hangover. So much for easy trips to sunny L.A.

As a result of becoming a friend of Jack Giroud, I immediately had law enforcement friends all over the State of California and the United States. Jack had a personal motto: "Police helping Police." He lived that motto, and I learned to do the same. As a county detective, I had reasons to go to California on several occasions. If those trips ever involved the L.A. area, I always had a driver named Jack.

Jack welcomed us into his world. He and others had formed the California Robbery Investigators Association (C.R.I.A.) Jack was already known as "Mr. Robbery" throughout California law enforcement agencies. C.R.I.A. is still a very active and successful group that has been instrumental in the training and networking of detectives for more than fifty years. I joined the California Robbery Investigators Association and soon had friends in most of the major police departments in the State of California.

I met a lot of California V.I.P.s in the world of law enforcement. These included Daryl Gates, the beloved chief of police in L.A., and several of L.A.'s district attorneys, including Steve Cooley. The number of times my relationship with Jack Giroud helped my career and made my investigative world more productive are too many to mention.

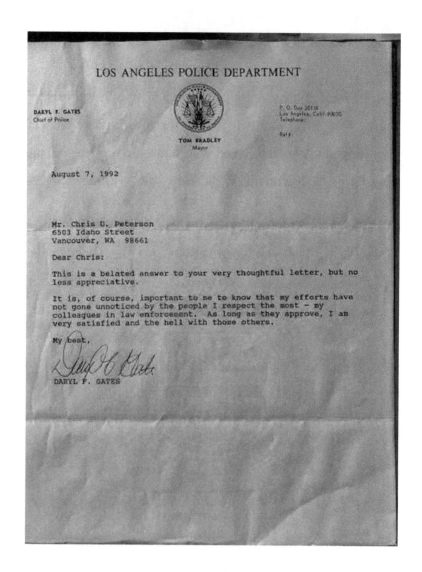

LOS ANGELES POLICE DEPARTMENT

DARYL F. GATES
Chief of Police

TOM BRADLEY
Mayor

P. O. Box 30158
Los Angeles, Calif. 90030
Telephone:

Ref #:

August 7, 1992

Mr. Chris D. Peterson
6503 Idaho Street
Vancouver, WA 98661

Dear Chris:

This is a belated answer to your very thoughtful letter, but no
less appreciative.

It is, of course, important to me to know that my efforts have
not gone unnoticed by the people I respect the most - my
colleagues in law enforcement. As long as they approve, I am
very satisfied and the hell with those others.

My best,

DARYL F. GATES

Chief Daryl Gates, one of the true leaders in modern law enforcement.

MEXICAN DRUG CONNECTION

Years after meeting Jack, I was assigned to the Regional
Organized Crime Network (R.O.C.N.) in Portland. I spent
from 1990-1994 in this highly significant dope unit.
R.O.C.N. became aware that a couple of Boeing employees

were muling dope for the Mexican cartels from Los Angeles, CA, to Seattle, WA. It was a Sunday when we made the traffic stop on I-5 near Wilsonville, OR, and found a kilo or two of cocaine in the suspect's vehicle. At the time, that was a significant amount of contraband. The couriers told us where they had obtained the drugs, and they said there was more cocaine and several guns at that residence in California. Despite overtime budget issues, by 4:00 p.m. that Sunday afternoon, L.A.P.D. narcotics officers were executing a search warrant on the residence where a large number of drugs, money, and guns were seized, thanks to Jack.

COPS HELPING COPS

A female F.B.I. agent in Portland, who was a good friend, told me of her frustration with the local F.B.I. office in L.A. Her complaint was that she could not get their assistance in a timely fashion. I told her that I would make a call to L.A. and get her what she needed. A short time later, she was flying to L.A., and the issue was solved within hours. Thank you, "Jackie" Giroud, for "Cops helping Cops," and thank you to that Utah farm boy robber who indirectly introduced me to Jack in the first place.

When Jack Giroud retired from the L.A.P.D. in 2007, he had fifty-one years and three months on the job. All the local notables were present for his retirement. This included Chief Bratton, former Chief Daryl Gates, and Steve Cooley, the long-time L.A. District Attorney. A county judge was the acting master of ceremonies. The large auditorium at the L.A. Police Academy was overflowing. It was one of the most memorable experiences of my life.

Jack Giroud, LAPD retirement caricature

BOOM BOOM

I also became lifelong friends with several of Jack's partners. One of the most notable was Ray "Boom Boom" Hernandez. Ray worked homicide and robbery for many years. One of the funniest short stories about Boom Boom came from his retirement. When one retires from the L.A.P.D., there is normally a caricature drawn of them with notes like dates where they were assigned, when they were hired, and when they retired. In Boom Boom's case, his caricature was different. It showed him shaped like the bowling ball he was with his shoes on, but there was one sock missing.

Being a highly trained investigator, I inquired several times about Boom Boom wearing only one sock. One day, I received an honest, no B.S. answer. Boom Boom was working a kidnapping case in a barrio of L.A. When he was staked out in the victim's home, he had to go to number two, but there was no toilet paper available. Yup, you guessed it; he used one of his socks to wipe with.

Many years after meeting Jack, I was working with a well-known Portland Detective, Cheryl Kanzler. One day Cheryl said to me, "You are the best-connected detective I know." When Cheryl told me this, it was a source of pride, but I knew who really deserved that compliment. Law

Enforcement lost a bigger-than-life hero when Jack Giroud passed away in 2019.

Ray Hernandez LAPD "Boom Boom" retirement caricature

Chapter 8

UNIFORM: 1978-1981

Almost half of my police career was spent driving a patrol car in high-crime areas, and I enjoyed it. In Multnomah County, being a detective was not a promotion but rather a rotation. Thus, there were times between detective assignments when I was driving a "sled" or "prowl car" on the street. This was a bit unusual, as most law enforcement agencies had a specific detective rank. That policy was likely in place so that more officers could experience being a detective, but I feel that this approach to policing was ill-advised.

One of the things that makes a successful patrol officer is getting out of your car. Other cops and some of my bosses used to criticize me for spending too much time in bars and restaurants. I consider myself guilty as charged. No one ever solved a crime sitting in their prowl car, answering police calls, and listening to the F.M. radio stations. My time getting to know the owners and patrons of the local establishments on my beat helped me solve many cases. I made a lot of arrests over the years based on information gained during my time sitting in a coffee shop or a bar visiting with members of the community.

STEREO SUPER STORES: MIKE MCGETTIGAN

Early in my career, a Portland business named Stereo Super Stores was burglarized. The owner was Mike McGettigan. Garry Christensen and I were assigned to that burglary case. Within a short time, we arrested the janitor in the mall where the business was located. Mike appreciated our work, and I became close friends with him and his girlfriend, Sherry.

BAJA CALIFORNIA/ MEXICO

Mike invited me to spend some time on his boat in LaPaz, Mexico fishing in the Sea of Cortez. On our first trip down there, my wife Diana and I stayed at Mike's house for a few days while he was coming back to port from a fishing trip. That was when we discovered that the whole world did not speak English. We couldn't communicate with Mike's housekeeper, the store employees, or anyone else in town. I had taken Spanish in high school and college, so my vocabulary was pretty basic. This language barrier has changed a lot in LaPaz over the last forty years. Since then, English has become more widely spoken, especially in tourist areas.

LEARNING SPANISH

This trip was my inspiration to expand my Spanish, and I started working on it "poco a poco." Shortly after that, Bud Johnson and I caught a homicide where the victim was a Mexican from Cabo San Lucas, and two of the three suspects in the case only spoke Spanish. Listening to the interpreter as best I could, reminded me that I needed to learn this language. I started taking Spanish classes, studying with friends, and going out of my way to speak with Mexican farm workers that I came across in my police work. I started assisting in classes taught by Catholic Charities, which helped immigrants pass the driving test. It wasn't too long before Mexican families in the county started inviting me to their kids' birthday parties. The office designated me as the Hispanic Affairs Officer, and just like that, I was off and running with my Spanish. Multnomah County sent me to a short Spanish immersion school in Cuernavaca, Mexico. Some years later, I enrolled in a language school in Puerto Vallarta, Mexico.

One of the issues for Mexicans trusting police officers is the fact that law enforcement in Mexico is largely for sale. With that fact in mind, language skills in Spanish go a long way toward gaining the confidence of Spanish speakers in the United States. This language school in Mexico changed my life in many ways. I fell in love with Puerto Vallarta and have had many opportunities to visit the area over the course of my life, both as a tourist and a private investigator.

I got to know my beat in S.E. Portland, as well as the cop character did in Joseph Wambaugh's book *The Blue Knight*. There were two major streets that ran through my district: Division and Powell. I have already mentioned Johnny Chin, the seventy-year-old restaurant owner with his meat cleaver who owned The New Cathay on Division St. The following are some other characters that I met during my time working in East Multnomah County.

NAKED WOMAN IN CORBETT

I got a call one day from Corbett, a small community in East Multnomah County. It was still early in the afternoon, and the call was simply this: "A naked woman sitting on the street in Corbett." I did not hurry, as it wasn't an emergency. I assumed the woman would be gone when I arrived twenty minutes later, but much to my surprise, she was still there and quite naked. This twenty-year-old woman was obviously on drugs; she had evidently discovered the joys of living better through chemistry. She was both gorgeous and cooperative. I finally got her into the back seat of my patrol car and gave her a wool blanket to cover up. We left for the county hospital, but the blanket didn't stay on very long. When I was crossing the Marquam bridge going into downtown Portland, I could see that this situation was providing a lot of entertainment for all the truckers. They were looking down at us and talking on their C.B. radios, so I was glad that the hospital was close. When we arrived, I wrapped my friend in the blanket again and walked her into the hospital E.R. She was in handcuffs, and the medical staff quickly reprimanded me for having her shackled. The cuffs came off, and my new friend was placed into an exam room alone. Moments later, the proverbial shit hit the fan as all the loose items in the exam room became airborne. No one but me seemed to notice the bedlam, so I went into the room. Seconds later, an E.R. nurse came in and said, "You can't be in here, this woman is naked." This whole situation seemed pretty ironic, seeing as how I had driven her in this same condition all the way from Corbett to downtown. Whatever!

THE GROVE

The Grove was a bar at 112th and SE Powell St. in Portland. I got to know the second-generation owner Jim McKee pretty well during this time. The Grove was a lively night spot run by world-class folks, and it would often be one of my first coffee stops on my afternoon shift. Lots of good stories came from the Grove. It was a blue-collar bar in a working-class neighborhood. Men were the predominant customers in the bar after work hours. One afternoon while I was having my coffee, I saw a bar regular named John getting ready to leave. It appeared that John had drunk too much, so I politely suggested that he not drive. I told him in my least authoritarian voice that if he let me finish my coffee, I would give him a ride home. John happily agreed.

Several months later, at the Grove, John asked if he could talk to me in private for a moment. He told me that there had been two customers in the bar earlier, and they were spending a lot of silver dollars and silver certificates: not the usual currency of local patrons. He suspected that the money was probably stolen. Evidently, the two guys had left the bar, but they came back just moments later. The pair asked John to help jump their car, as the battery was dead. When the car still wouldn't start, they asked John to give them a ride home which he did. Prior to leaving, he told me that the two men had dumped some papers near the parking lot.

John took me to the discarded papers, and I examined them. The address on the documents was nearby, so I went to speak with the occupant, an Asian lady with limited English skills. She explained that her residence had recently been burglarized. I contacted the on-duty detectives, and a short time later, the suspects were arrested for the burglary. This story is one of many prime examples explaining why I got my butt out of the car and talked to the "neighbors" who paid my wages.

One weekend night, I went into the Grove in uniform to get a cup of coffee and say hello to the employees and owners. I was standing at the end of the bar visiting with the bartender, when a patron started hassling me. There was no doubt that his judgment was impaired. I was in uniform and well-liked in the club. I warned the guy a couple of times to back off and shut up. I was really trying to ignore him, as I did not need the hassle. The place was packed with a live band playing onstage, but all of a sudden, the music stopped. Glenn Cass, the singer and guitarist asked over the microphone, "Deputy Peterson are you having a problem?" Shortly after that, the "problem" faded away. This is what police work should look like in our country.

Unfortunately, that is not the case today.

Over the course of my policing career, I would often stop at local bars and visit while drinking a coffee or soda. One of my funny memories from this time was Sgt. Guy Moore called over the radio to meet up with me at one of my local bar stops called The Flower Drum. The "Drum," as locals called it, was located at 145th and S.E. Division St. Sgt. Moore met me in the bar's parking lot and got uncomfortably close to my face when talking to me. It was clear that someone had called the office and reported that a uniformed deputy was sitting and drinking at the bar. Sgt. Moore did what he needed to do, and I reassured him that no one would ever catch me sitting at a bar in uniform drinking alcohol. I did, however, continue visiting these local establishments to drink my usual non-alcoholic beverage of choice.

There was a restaurant at 104th and SE Holgate St. that I spent a fair amount of time in. To the public, I probably looked like a lazy cop who loved to drink coffee and eat. While both of those descriptions seemed accurate, they couldn't have been farther from the truth. Big Al Pasinetti used to be in there a lot. He came up to me one day and said there was a lot of drug dealing going on at the house next door to where he lived. Al was a big Sicilian, and he made it clear that he would take matters into his own hands if law enforcement did not deal with the problem. Al had two young boys, and he did not want them exposed to this type of situation. Based on Al's information, the Portland Police Bureau arrested a number of ex-cons and recovered a lot of stolen guns from his duplicitous next-door neighbors.

THE MAVERICK

There was a bar and restaurant known as the Maverick at 125th and S.E. Division St. owned by Steve Fackrell, who was the second-generation owner. His employees loved us, and they always treated cops well. One day I was eating at the counter in uniform when Steve Fackrell sat down beside me. He discreetly pulled an antique revolver out of a sock and showed it to me. The gun appeared to be valuable, and I asked him where he got it. He told me that he bought it from a customer named Steve Bridgeman, who had a gold and silver buying business nearby.

Fackrell and I went into his office at the Maverick, and I ran a check on the gun to see if it was stolen. Long story short, it was. Using this information, I recovered a large number of guns that had been stolen from a collector's home. I did a bit of research and learned that Steve Bridgeman was in the Federal Witness Protection Program. He had been involved in a large narcotics investigation on the East Coast, but it seemed that he was unable to put his life of crime behind him. The owner of the guns was overjoyed and bought me dinner one night. Bridgeman had purchased the stolen guns from this burglary, no doubt.

STEVE BRIDGEMAN

About that same time, I heard from many locals that Bridgeman was using lots of cocaine and making all sorts of bad decisions. Shortly after the gun incident, he disappeared. He had sprayed a house at 6642 SE Knight St. with bullets, and his Mercedes was found abandoned nearby. Bridgemen previously told my partner Denny Branagan that the house he shot at belonged to his cocaine connection. It appeared that Steve's actual name was Steven Douglas King.

I knew a local musician who had since passed away named Billie Sampson. Sampson came to me one day and said he feared that Bridgeman might have been murdered. Although he could not confirm the death, he told me that Bridgeman had tried to hire him to kill a man named Lee. Billie said Lee was a pimp, and he was fighting with Bridgemen over a female. This was just another chaotic day in Bridgeman's life.

When Bridgeman went missing, Denny Branagan and I did some poking around, but we couldn't find out if he ran off or was killed. We visited a house on Regner Rd. in Gresham, where Bridgeman used to live. The landlady said that the front door had been kicked in, and the house was ransacked. The landlady's daughter was now living there. Upon moving in, she found some cocaine and marijuana in the house, which she promptly burned in the fireplace.

Years later, in 2002, a person contacted Det. Gary Muncy from the sheriff's office and told him that she had been present in a house when Bridgeman was murdered. Since this person was a confidential informant in a case that is still open, we will refer to her as Tammy from here on. Muncy was working cold cases at the time. Tammy could not provide detailed information regarding the day and year of this occurrence, but she did know that Bridgemen was involved in the drug trade with his killers.

Tammy said that she was at a house when Bridgeman arrived demanding cocaine to freebase. The men in the house sent Tammy to a bedroom and told her not to come out, no matter what. When she asked what was going to happen, the men said, "We are going to kill him." Tammy thought this must be a joke, but moments later, she heard Bridgeman pleading for his life, screaming, "Please don't kill me!" After many minutes of screaming, the two men told Tammy to open the door that she had locked. She reluctantly came out and saw both men sweating and breathing hard. One of them was covered with blood, but she couldn't remember what the second one looked like.

The living room area had blood, hair, tissue, and brain matter on the walls and ceiling.

Bridgeman was not present. The men told Tammy that they had beaten Bridgemen with pieces of firewood to the extent that his brains were coming out of his head. They also told her that he was clutching his crack pipe during the assault, which one of the men found to be very funny.

Tammy was told to clean up the mess while the men left in two cars, one of which was Bridgeman's Mercedes. Tammy stayed at the house until the suspects returned; she was afraid to leave for fear of getting killed. She also stayed around to take advantage of the cocaine that was readily available. Three days later, the men returned with coins and jewelry that they had stolen from Bridgeman's home since he had been in the business of buying gold and silver. All of the players in this event were heavily addicted to cocaine. I had heard all kinds of stories about Bridgeman's craziness as a cocaine addict, and it clearly did not work out well for him in the end.

To my knowledge, this case has never been solved, even though it now appears that one of the suspects has likely been identified. Unfortunately, the confidential informant, Tammy, didn't make a good witness, as she was heavily addicted to drugs, and most of the evidence disappeared in the ensuing years. Tammy did tell Det. Muncy that the men had allegedly put Bridgeman's body in a sleeping bag that was weighted down and threw it into the Willamette River near Oregon City. The body has never been recovered.

This episode shows just how much lawlessness drug addiction can lead to. The thought that society might want to decriminalize drugs is appalling to me. How many people have died by overdose or murder; how many families have been destroyed; how many children are not being raised by their biological parents due to the ramifications of drug addiction?

MAVERICK: UNWANTED DRUNK

One of my favorite Maverick stories was related to an "unwanted drunk call." I had my neighbor Hans Johnson riding along with me. Hans was finishing up his Ph.D., and I think the ride along was a chance for him to take a break from his studies. We arrived at the Maverick a short time after receiving the call. One of the waitresses named Laurie was standing by the curb. She pointed to a set of tail lights headed East on Division St. and said, "That's him. Since he's gone, we're okay."

I followed the tail lights and caught up with the car as it pulled into the Pink Feather, which was the next bar on the street. As I watched the car, it was obvious that the driver was under the influence. When he got out of his car, I saw a small man with a big mouth. After getting the needed documents from him, I realized that he was a truck driver, and a drunk driving ticket would be a game changer for him and his career. I asked him if he had a dime, as that was the cost of a call from a phone booth at the time. He started in on me and wanted to know why he needed a dime. I explained it a couple of times, telling him to call a family member so they could come to pick him up. Finally, I got frustrated and told him to get into my backseat and that I would give him a ride home. Even though he only lived a

94

couple of miles away, I was doing him a big favor by not citing him.

I drove him home, and when he got to his front porch, he turned in my direction and gave me the finger. I had seen another car in his driveway and told him not to get into that car and drive. Half an hour later, Hans and I were parked by an intersection, and I saw the drunk go by in his second car. So… he ended up getting arrested for drunk driving after all.

Several months later, I got a subpoena to show up for a trial on this guy. I thought, what moron attorney would take this one to court? I showed up and was really looking forward to the trial. The defendant saw me in the hallway and told his attorney that I was present. His attorney promptly went into the judge's chambers and entered a guilty plea. I guess they were hoping I wouldn't show up and the charges would be dismissed. This situation is a good example of why cops might develop an attitude when dealing with unruly suspects.

COPS: A SUMMER WITH THE CREW

The show *COPS,* which began in the '80s, was produced by Barbour/Langley Productions out of Hollywood, CA. The first episodes were filmed in Florida and New Orleans, but then they came to the Multnomah County Sheriff's Office to film. They spent a summer with M.C.S.O., and a lot of the filming was with the county narcotics unit, which was headed by Sgt. John Bunnell at the time.

John became a national figure during these years. Much of the time *COPS* spent with John showed one of the most effective drug units in the country. I was proud of this fact. There were a number of huge cases highlighted to the nation, but some downsides came along with this attention as well. One of those pitfalls was that John exposed a valuable tool to the underworld: the "body wire." It looked like a pager which, before cell phones, was a major tool of the drug dealer's trade. John was demonstrating this device to an officer while the T.V. cameras were rolling. This seemingly tiny detail infuriated dope cops around the country. If an undercover cop was discovered wearing a wire, his life would most certainly be in jeopardy. John survived this oversight and even became the Multnomah County Sheriff for a time before focusing on the entertainment world. He had his own show called *Police Chases*, produced by Paul Stojanovich, who was also with Barbour/Langley Productions.

Photo taken by friend John Campbell

The higher-ups in the department picked the uniformed officers that they wanted to partner with *COPS*. I assumed those picked were known for their work ethic or had beats that were in high-crime areas. I was picked to appear on the show, and it turned into a fun summer, to say the least.

SGT. LOREN CADDY

Sgt. Loren Caddy was picked to host a *COPS* crew. Although I rotated in and out of uniform at various times in my career, I had already worked with him many times in my eight years at the department. A lot of his segments were seen on national T.V., as were mine. Loren and I remain close to this day, like brothers, even now, after many years of retirement. I still address him as Sgt. Caddy when I speak to him on the phone, albeit with a smile.

Sgt. Loren Caddy, MCSO - Our Fearless Leader

Loren grew up in Scappoose, Oregon. He was a tall, good-looking man who had a reputation for being well-liked by his co-workers and the community. In high school, he was a star athlete and a well-renowned singer in various bands. He upheld the epitome of hard work and decency. When the *COPS* crew rode with us that summer, they spent a lot of time with Loren. As a result of being seen on *COPS*, the county created life-like cutouts of Loren and me, which were displayed at the Multnomah County Fair that year. I have a photo of my wife Diana standing between our cutouts at the fair. She loves Loren as much as I do.

Diana Peterson between Loren Caddy and Chris Peterson cutouts displayed

But I digress. Occasionally, as a police officer, you end up dealing with someone so obnoxious that you know it won't end well. Nobody wants to do something that will get them sent to the office. I had a good remedy to this problem in my years working with Loren. When I was dealing with an obnoxious asshole, I would say, "I suggest you speak with my sergeant." They would almost always say something like, "You're damn right. I want to speak with your sergeant."

I would then get on my radio, call for 171, which was my supervisor's call sign, and proceed to tell Loren that a citizen wanted to speak with him. Being a responsible sergeant and stuck with me as a subordinate, he would quickly respond. I then politely introduced the good citizen to Loren, jumped in my prowl car, and took my leave. If I didn't drive away too quickly, I could often see Loren vigorously tapping his finger on the complainant's chest. Sometimes I would just send the unhappy party to his office for discussions about their concerns.

Throughout my career, Loren would invariably give me that "look" when I saw him later.

My response was generally, "Loren, you make a dollar an hour more than me; suck it up." To say that Loren cared about those who worked for him would be an understatement. The Lesson here is simple: if something is above your pay grade in life, don't be embarrassed to send it to a higher authority. Most of those obnoxious folks forgot that they had ever met me, and for that, I love you, Loren!

The *COPS* crew that I worked with consisted of John Campbell on camera and Brett Grant-Grierson as the sound man. John was from Portland, and Brett was from South Africa. The cameras and sound equipment were big and bulky, but we somehow got everyone and everything into my prowl car. We spent countless numbers of hours together.

We would show up at the ugly moments in many people's lives, and the equipment would start rolling to record the scene. Those being filmed acted like this was a common occurrence and continued beating their wives or fighting the neighbors with impunity. They didn't question the presence of the crew, and if they objected later, their faces would be digitized: no one would be able to identify them. As I think about my early interest in *Dragnet* and Joe Friday with his partner throwing peanut shells out the window while on surveillance, my experiences are much more vivid, violent, and fast-moving.

SKINNY HYPE IN BIKINI

Several of my segments with *COPS* ultimately aired on National T.V. and those episodes are still played periodically or available online. My district was an epicenter of drug use and poverty. One of the segments that made it past the cutting room floor involved a single father with two pre-teen children. When we arrived at the scene, he showed me some used hypodermic needles on the street in front of his house. My recollection is that the man had recently relocated to Portland from Montana. What he was seeing was foreign and deeply troubling to him. I suspect this man was having the same reaction I had when I left my wonderful, bucolic Eastern Washington home only to realize that there were huge differences between the rural West and the bigger cities.

The man believed that the drug problems were coming from a residence several houses to his West. He had recently experienced a conflict with the occupants of the said residence, and they had threatened to burn down his home. The look of despair on this man's face was palpable as he realized he had brought his children into a living hell as he saw it.

After a bit of investigation, I realized that a female in her twenties seemed to be the biggest source of concern. I found her at the Maverick at 125th and S.E. Division St. wearing a nasty-looking bikini. I arrested her and sent her off to jail. She might have weighed one hundred pounds soaking wet. Her appearance told me that she was likely an addict, or as I like to call it, living better through chemistry. This particular *COPS* episode has aired a number of times on National T.V., and it depicts me putting this tiny, skinny, unpleasant person into the back seat of a police car in handcuffs. So much for my macho image. As I write this, there is a political movement that wants to end the war on drugs. Don't buy into it. The drug culture is ugly, and it will destroy the America I've always loved.

My Cameraman, John Campbell, lived in Portland. I got to know John well, as I watched him closely while working together. I could sense his despair as he saw Portland and my district through the camera's lens. John was creative and used his talent to produce the show in a way that was real and accurate. One day I was driving West on S.E. Division St. as the sun was setting. John and his camera were in the front seat with me. All of a sudden, John yelled, "Chris, Stop!" My immediate thought was, "What did I miss?" I quickly stopped as instructed. John got out with his 35 MM camera and took a photo of a large red and yellow neon sign. It was advertising one of the many cheap motels in the area, known as the Division Street Motel. I had driven past the sign hundreds of times and never saw anything attractive about it. John saw a beautiful sunset in the clouds surrounding a loud, garish sign. The photo has graced my desk for over thirty-five years. I didn't see what John saw. All I saw was a place where I had arrested a number of felons over the years. Rest in Peace, John.

Photo taken by John Campbell, COPS Crew. The colors caught his eye.

TRIPLE HOMICIDE – DYING DECLARATION

Probably the most dramatic event with *COPS* was a triple homicide that occurred while I was working in uniform. A call came in about a shooting. When I arrived at the location, there were two deceased Mexican females and a male victim who was also Mexican. He was still alive in the apartment but did not speak much English. The male

104

survivor was put in an ambulance where paramedics could treat his critical injuries. I entered the ambulance and started asking him questions. He might have been the last person able to explain what had just happened at the crime scene. I got what is called a "dying declaration" from this victim. This was probably one of the few dying declarations ever obtained on videotape, and the *COPS* crew captured it. A dying declaration is one of the exceptions to hearsay in a court of law. In this circumstance, the person who made the statement could not testify in court, and the statement was made with the belief that death was imminent. The statement must be relative to the pending death.

The dying declaration was given in Spanish, and I had to decipher it using my very limited Spanish vocabulary. The victim told me who the killer was, and we were quickly able to let law enforcement know which suspect to look for. There was, unfortunately, some confusion, as several witnesses provided a description of a person seen running from the area. Ironically, the person running should have been the fourth victim, and he was escaping the shooter. All of the people involved, both victims and shooters, were Mexicans. After an extensive search, we found the runner several blocks away. A neighbor had allowed him to come into his home and hide.

As it turned out, the massacre involved a love triangle. The runner spoke no English, but despite my very limited Spanish, I was able to obtain many needed details within an hour of the killings. All of this was filmed by the *COPS* crew, and it became a part of the Federal Language Training program in Glencoe, Georgia, which is a major training center for law enforcement in the U.S. It was not presented as an example of fluent Spanish, but it showed how important some Spanish ability could be to law enforcement. Sadly, the suspect escaped back to Mexico. Despite the efforts of federal law enforcement to locate and extradite him, he has never been arrested. Little did I know that many years later, I would find myself doing private investigations in Mexico.

Working uniform patrol had a lot of sad and funny moments. At Christmastime, we would have a bet in the roll call room before hitting the streets. The person that won the bet was the first officer who got a call, only to find a recently decorated Christmas tree lying in the front yard of a house. Such is the life of a policeman. The tree lying in the front yard was always related to a family fight. What a terrible way for children to experience the holidays.

Chapter 9

STING PROJECT: 1982-1984

In the early '80s, the Multnomah County Sheriff's Office received several federal grants to conduct undercover investigations or "sting projects." These covert operations were some of the most successful in the nation. My partner during this period was Bobbie Peterson, who I'd like to call a "super cop." Bob worked for the Gresham Police Department, but he was on loan to M.C.S.O. for many years. When it came to undercover work, Bob was the most effective guy I ever had the pleasure of working with. He had gut instincts like no one else.

Bobbie Peterson, Gresham PD - all-time great detective.

At the beginning of these undercover projects, we set up a tavern in Felony Flats on SE 82nd Ave. Felony Flats was also known as the Squirrel and Errol Heights.

We had cameras set up in the bar and recorded countless interactions buying stolen property and dope. After the county shut down the original tavern, it was named the "Sting" by the new owners. I'd call that poetic justice.

Working undercover, we rented houses and would bring crooks into our so-called home to buy all types of stolen property and dope. We had a van with a periscope camera and recorded our illegal "buys" all over the Portland metropolitan area. At one time, during a sting, we had a floating home on the Columbia River with a ski boat and all the accouterments.

UNDERCOVER IN HILLSBORO

In 1981 and 1982, Bob Peterson and I were assigned to the Special Enforcement Detail. This effort was largely funded by the federal government in the form of grants. There were officers from many different Oregon law enforcement branches, including Hillsboro, Washington County, Gresham, and the Oregon State Police. The Federal Law Enforcement Administration funded over sixty "sting" projects in the United States during this time. Sgt. John Bunnell of the Multnomah County Sheriff's Office was the main supervisor during this project, and he was one of the most imaginative cops I have ever worked with. Our unit was near the top in terms of production and positive results.

Undercover work was fascinating for a number of reasons. No one ever wrote the book on the correct way to perform this type of work. For those of us who were effective, it was mostly gut instinct stuff. Oftentimes an informant or a concerned citizen would give you what you needed to get started: i.e., an introduction. I remember sitting in a bar in the Squirrel one night, and after a few beers, a Mexican started telling me how he could get a lot of marijuana delivered from South of the border. In other words, there is a lot of bullshit ability involved. For cops who do not have that B.S. ability, undercover work is not all that smooth or effective.

One year we recovered millions of dollars' worth of stolen property and contraband. We arrested dozens of criminals. Virtually all of the operations that the unit engaged in required dedicated cooperation from every member and often involved long, difficult hours of surveillance, intelligence gathering, and extraordinary hard work by the entire unit. A lot of good "spy" equipment made us very effective. We also had significant support from federal grant money, which helped to enable our success.

Every day was an adventure. Bob and I spent a lot of time in rough bars all over the metro area.

We infiltrated a couple of bars that were hotbeds of criminal activity in the town of Hillsboro, about fifteen minutes West of Portland. I had befriended an ex-con named David R., and we spent a lot of time in these local establishments together. He had been locked up a number of times and was familiar with all of the city and county jails as well as the State Pen. Needless to say, he quickly fit in. One of the bars we frequented was a hub of vice; it was noted for illicit drug sales and gun trading. I befriended the bartender, and before long, I was buying stolen guns and dope. At the end of this project, the bartender was arrested and prosecuted.

On another night in a different bar in Hillsboro, I took my former partner Garry Christensen with me, as I did not feel comfortable going into these places by myself. This particular establishment was notorious for being a rough spot. As Garry and I were sitting at the bar drinking beer, a random guy got up and hit another patron so hard that he fell off of his barstool onto the floor. Garry's reaction was the same one that most cops would have. He jumped up to confront the assailant. I quickly grabbed Garry, unbeknownst to the crowd around us. I quietly told him to sit down, explaining that this was a regular occurrence and we weren't in there to be bouncers.

I was officially on duty. However, Garry wasn't. He had just gone along to keep me company. Garry was acting as a normal cop would, but I had spent a lot of time in Hillsboro trying to infiltrate several rough bars. Acting like a cop would have blown my cover and likely destroyed a lot of the progress I had made. Many times, while working undercover, a police officer will have to pretend that he is on the wrong side of the law. There were times when we did not even want to have a badge in our possession. There were times when a badge could get you killed.

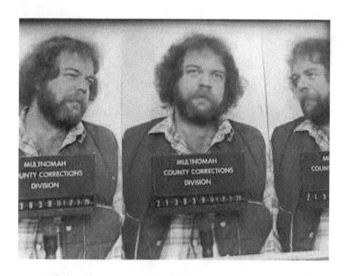

Chris Peterson MCSO undercover mug shot.

DO YOU WANT TO SEE MY TURKEYS?

One day, the Oregon State Police (O.S.P.) contacted my boss, John Bunnell, and asked him to send a couple of guys to Pacific City, Oregon, where a burglary had been committed involving a large number of chainsaws. My partner, for a brief period of time, was an O.S.P. trooper. We went to Pacific City to get acquainted and see what we could learn. We were in a bar that was mostly occupied by loggers, commercial fishermen, and guys who split cedar shakes for a living. Splitting cedar shakes is the way that cedar rounds are split to make cedar shingles. It is rough work, and folks who do it for a living are very likely tough individuals in a physical sense. I heard my partner, who had overindulged, say something stupid to a guy who split shakes for a living. When my partner was out of earshot for a moment, I told the guy that I would buy him a beer if he would just leave my buddy alone. I then managed to get my partner out of the bar to our motel, where he was safe from himself. This particular partner did not handle his alcohol well, so I did not like working undercover with him. The protocol for working undercover allowed us to drink while on duty. This, of course, would not have been permitted for uniformed officers or detectives. If a police officer working undercover got into an accident while under the influence, the penalty would have been severe.

I went back to the bar and was soon one of the crowd. At closing time, the shake splitter asked me if I wanted to go to his house for breakfast. It was about 2:30 a.m., so of course, I said yes, and away we went into the coastal mountain range near Hebo, Oregon. While this seemed all good and fine, I was still on the job and in search of the stolen chainsaws. We arrived at this guy's mountain cabin, and he promptly woke his wife up, saying, "Get up and fix breakfast; we have company." This situation was getting really dangerous, as there was nothing more perilous than waking a sleeping woman at 2:30 a.m. and demanding that she cook for a stranger.

While she was laboring away, my new friend asked, "Do you want to see my turkeys?" Again I said yes and naturally expected to go outside. I quickly realized that this wasn't the case as he pulled the folding steps down from the attic and up the steps we went. There they were, about two dozen half-grown turkeys running around in the attic, just a few feet from the kitchen stove down below. I never found the chainsaws, but I quickly realized how dangerous this undercover work could be watching those turkeys dancing in the attic, mere feet away from the oven.

FAMILY BEEF

I had worked undercover in the Burglary Tactical Unit for quite some time before this particular sting. While this type of investigative work is tentative, I was becoming quite good at undercover policing. From April 1981 - March 1982, I spent the majority of my time working undercover with Bob Peterson. We worked out of a building that had been the Multnomah County Poor Farm years earlier. No one who looked like a cop ever showed up at this location, so it was safe for undercover officers. If there were obvious signs of law enforcement activity around this building, it could have immediately created a problem for us. There was a warehouse on the property where we stored stolen cars and all kinds of "acquired" property. This location later became the famous Portland area landmark known as McMenamins Edgefield in Troutdale, OR.

I will provide an example of trying to keep undercover operations out of the public view and why that is important.

One day Bobbie Peterson and I were leaving the Edgefield area in an undercover vehicle. Bobbie and I had just started working together, so we were still getting acquainted. He was just a few years out of the navy, and I was just a few years out of the air force. Bobbie was a Gresham police officer.

As we drove by a nearby track, Bobbie saw a jogger running laps. He told me to stop the car and immediately grabbed his 35 MM camera with a telephoto lens and started taking photos of the jogger. He said, "That is Steve Kessler." I had no idea who Kessler was at that point but soon learned that he was one of the most dangerous crooks in Oregon with a reputation for violence. We would both get to know Kessler and his crimes better at a future date.

While I was still in uniform, just prior to being sent to the Special Enforcement Detail or the Sting Project, I got called to a local house on a domestic violence case that involved a family beef. As events unfolded on this particular call, there was a significant interaction between myself and the man who lived there. Ironically, a couple of weeks later, I was invited into this same house while undercover. I immediately recognized the man and woman, but they didn't recognize me. My appearance had changed considerably during that time, as I didn't shave or cut my hair. Ultimately, I purchased my first stolen car and some dope from them.

Months later, as we were wrapping up the project, I went to that house with other officers to make the arrest. I had a little plastic badge on my shirt which said, "It has been fun, but you are under arrest." I still remember feeling a bit uncomfortable when I made the arrest. I had gotten to know the man, and although he had done some bad things, I still felt compassion for him. I had those kinds of pangs several times during my undercover days. While in most cases, these crises of conscience don't affect me, sometimes they ring true. This is especially the case when the people involved aren't evil at heart but have simply made a series of bad decisions.

SPOIL YOUR VACATION – CAMPGROUND PROWLER

In September of 1981, Bob Peterson and I arrested a career criminal named Mark Harold Huddleston. We became aware of Huddleston through other law enforcement officers. Huddleston was well known throughout the country as a cat burglar who prowled campgrounds at night looking for purses and anything else of value. He was particularly well known in California to the federal and state park rangers, but he lived in Gresham, OR with his wife.

We executed a search on a storage locker in Gresham that Huddleston was using. Among other items found were $25,000 worth of cameras. He also later turned over $40,000 worth of stolen money orders and a large number of stolen credit cards. We were able to connect him to many of the thefts by matching up where the crimes occurred and then looking at the location of the phone calls that he made home to his wife. When the two matched up, we knew he was a likely suspect. I was able to locate a great number of victims across the Southern tier of the United States. Huddleston and his fellow crooks had a unique approach to their crimes. They would enter the campgrounds waiting for dark to start stealing items. They often walked around these campgrounds in stocking feet to be quieter.

After a full night of stealing, the crew would leave the campground early in the morning with a lot of stolen property and credit cards. One of their first stops would be large retail outlets for spending sprees and buying high-value items. Many of the purchased goods had been specifically pre-ordered by the crook's "customers" who wanted certain cameras, stereos, or other expensive electronics. Not wanting to risk using the credit cards once they were reported as stolen, these burglars would use them for an hour or two and then get rid of them.

Huddleston cooperated and was not prosecuted in this particular instance. One reason for this leniency was that he agreed to introduce Bobbie and me to twenty-five of his criminal associates while we were undercover. His many introductions led us to the most violent crime group in Oregon at that time. I spent a lot of time with Huddleston in 1981 and 1982.

He also agreed to meet with the federal and state park rangers who had been chasing him for years. The meeting took place in Pacific Grove, CA, in December of 1981, and I recorded it. Thus, many of his past activities were now documented. It was ironic that Huddleston drove to the meeting in his expensive Porsche. One might have thought that all this interaction with law enforcement would have scared him straight, but it did not. In 1982, he was arrested in the Great Smoky Mountains and sentenced to ten years in prison for burglary and assault after assaulting a park ranger.

Scared straight this time? Nope, you guessed it. After getting released from prison for the Great Smoky Mountains caper, he got arrested again. This time it was in Oregon in May of 1994. A task force initiated by the Santa Barbara County District Attorney's Office had been keeping watch on his felonious sojourns into campsites on the West Coast. At the time, he had in his possession thirty-seven hundred CDs, one-hundred-and-thirty-two watches, lots of jewelry, and other items linked to auto burglaries in Santa Barbara County campgrounds. In June of 1996, he was sentenced to twelve years in prison.

I interviewed Huddleston many times in 1981, often in the county jail. As a good detective will do, I developed a rapport with him and learned that we had a common interest in real estate. He even tried to get me to go into the real estate business with him when he got out of jail. After his 1994 arrest, due to the known rapport we had, I was asked to interview Huddleston again. I wasn't involved in this particular case, nor did I follow up on it. During this interview, I was struck by the poise and calm he exhibited while being questioned. In my 1996 letter to Judge William Gordon in Santa Barbara, I made the following comments: "Huddleston is a charming con-man who needs to be put away. I am convinced that he never had a legitimate source of income in his life."

FAMOUS OUTLAW

One of the early big projects Bobbie and I worked on involved a local criminal named Stephen Kessler. Huddleston had facilitated our initial introduction to the Kessler crime family when he was cooperating with law enforcement in the early 80s. Kessler was a bit of a folk legend in the Portland underworld. He was associated with the worst of the worst and had a network of dope dealers and bank robbers. He had been intermittently locked up for long periods of time, but when he was free, there was inevitably a crime spree associated with him.

Huddleston had also introduced us to a couple of female drug dealers named Valerie and Tammy, and we had been buying small quantities of heroin from them. They were both addicts, selling just enough to feed their own habits. With a bit of luck, we learned that they were part of the Kessler organization. They were both low-level, but it was a start for us. We borrowed a D.M.V. machine from the state and told these women that we had a lot of stolen traveler's checks. We would furnish them with Oregon driver's licenses that they could use to cash the checks and then keep half of the proceeds.

We had recovered thousands of traveler's cheques that Huddleston and his friends had stolen in state and federal parks. We couldn't actually cash the stolen checks, so we would go to the bank and buy $500 worth of valid traveler's cheques. We would put these valid cheques in a pile on top of the stack of stolen ones. When the ladies were around, we would reach into the stack and hand them the cheques that we had purchased. We would then create a driver's license with their photo on it, and off they would go to cash a cheque and bring us back half of the proceeds.

The word soon got out that these ladies had some serious connections. During this undercover operation, we did not hide our guns, as we wanted the word out that we were bad guys. The plan worked, and soon enough, we were dealing with one of Kessler's lieutenants named Richard Ruip. Kessler had an outstanding warrant in Oregon, so he was using Ruip to deal heroin in Portland from his home up in Seattle, WA.

One night I was set up to buy an ounce of heroin from Ruip. I was in a cheap motel on SE 82nd Ave. in Portland, and we had surveillance watching Ruip in the hopes that we might catch sight of Kessler. I was backed up by several of my guys as well as three or four F.B.I. agents. Ruip went to a bar ten miles from my location in Troutdale and met with someone. The agent who watched the meeting take place could not tell who it was that Ruip was meeting with. We decided to drop the Ruip surveillance and dope buy to watch this other person hoping that it was Kessler. Although we weren't sure it was him, the man was headed in the right direction out of town towards Seattle.

Occasionally, truly funny things happen. There were eight or nine officers at the motel in adjoining rooms and also outside in vehicles. When it was decided to abort my narcotic's buy with Richard Ruip, we all started leaving in a hurry to head towards Troutdale so that we could be around if and when Kessler was arrested. As we were rapidly leaving, the motel manager heard the stampede. He looked out and saw all kinds of guns in our hands. He hollered, "I'm calling the police." I heard my friend Stan Renning from the F.B.I. yell, "We are the police."

We contacted the Washington State Patrol and made arrangements for them to do a traffic stop for us. The stop was made near Castle Rock, WA, on I-5, Northbound. Kessler pulled over but saw one of our unmarked cars nearby. He smelled a rat and took off. He went a short distance to Headquarters Rd. and took the exit. When he came to a stop at the top of the ramp, he came out shooting with two guns, barely missing the D.E.A. agent and trooper who were chasing him. Kessler ran from his car into the nearby woods.

This area was remote and heavily forested, so we could not find him in the dark. We searched for hours with no success. At one point, I was in a chopper that had been provided to us by a logging company. The man flying the helicopter had been an army pilot in Vietnam. The police on the ground were telling me that we needed to get the chopper down lower for better illumination. I relayed this information to the pilot, and he asked me what I thought. I said, "I do not want to get lower." I knew Kessler would love to add shooting at a chopper to his resume. I told the guys on the ground that we were not getting any lower. They told me to get the hell out of there because we were just bothering the search canines. Away we flew into the dark.

It was a cold winter night, and none of us, including Kessler, were dressed for the freezing wet conditions of this forest adjacent to I-5. About daylight, all of us dope cops gave up the search and headed back towards Portland. A couple of reserve police officers from Castle Rock P.D. arrested a cold and wet Kessler without incident later that morning.

JAILHOUSE ESCAPE & ATTEMPTED MURDER

Steve Kessler was extradited back to Oregon and booked into the Multnomah County Jail. Kessler was locked up with several of his long-time friends in NE Portland's Rocky Butte Jail. He had a history of escapes, attempted escapes, and other violent behavior. Kessler was also allegedly a member of the Aryan Brotherhood, which had a stronghold in Portland in the 80s.

On July 25th, 1982, at approximately 10 p.m., Steve Kessler showed the world what an animal he really was. A corrections officer had been "compromised" by a seriously bad inmate named Roger Allen, which resulted in the introduction of a gun into the jail. Allen had been allowed to go into an area of Rocky Butte Jail that was the entryway to A & B tanks. The A tank housed the inmates who were considered the most dangerous. The B tank housed disciplinary inmates. There was a total of thirteen single cells in maximum security.

That evening when Correction Officer Dunbar opened the door to the entryway, he found himself facing the gun that had been smuggled in. Dunbar was quickly tied up, and a group of visiting chaplains was also taken hostage and placed into cells. The doors to other cells were quickly unlocked, and there were now six inmates loose on the maximum-security floor. A short time later, Corrections Sgt. Jim Turney had just left the medical floor and was walking through the inmate mess hall. He came face to face with an armed Steve Kessler. Jim knew Kessler well, and his first thought was, "What the fuck is Kessler doing in civilian clothes?" Evidently, the chaplains had donated their clothing to the cause.

Jim found himself looking at the barrel of a small pistol in Kessler's hands. Kessler said, "Sergeant, this is loaded with dum-dums, and you know what they can do." Dum-dums are expanding bullets that produce a larger wound. Kessler ordered Jim Turney to walk towards the control room in front of him at gunpoint. This was the path to freedom for the escaping inmates. Jim was marched forward and told to put his face up against the window to the control room so that the officer outside would open the door when they saw him. What the guard outside could not see was the gun that had been placed up against Jim's head. Kessler banged on the door, and Deputy Irv Burkett saw the familiar face of Jim Turney, so he opened the door.

Jim was quickly shoved from behind, and now both staff and escapees were in the control room. A struggle ensued, and other inmates were fighting with Deputy Burkett. Kessler was distracted for a moment, so Jim grabbed for the gun. He was quickly knocked to the floor by the other inmates and then jerked to his feet and put in handcuffs. Irv Burkett broke free and grabbed for a radio, yelling, "Jailbreak!" Jim watched as Irv was lunging for the radio and saw Kessler track him with the pistol. He heard the gun go off, saw a puff of smoke, and then Irv crumbled to the floor. He had been shot in the head. Kessler manipulated the necessary toggle switches, and all six inmates went quickly into the wind. For the next week, there was a huge manhunt in the Portland area for the escapees. Kessler was not arrested in Portland but was subsequently apprehended out of state and brought back to Oregon. He spent the last thirty years of his life incarcerated and finally died in prison. Irv Burkett was nearing retirement when he was shot. He used to love hunting and fishing, but due to this brutal shooting, he lost most of his sight. He spent the rest of his life in a wheelchair or at the hospital. If it had not been for Irv's unbelievable will to live, this would have been a capital murder case.

I had been rotated back to uniform just before the jailbreak but was brought back into detectives to work on this case, as I was familiar with most of the escapees, particularly Kessler. Shortly after the escape, several of us visited the home of a woman who had been close to Kessler for a number of years. She lived near 84th and SE Burnside St. in Portland. At this particular moment, I was working once again with Denny Branagan and Bob Peterson.

The news media was monitoring our activities as best they could. This was a big case in the eyes of the local media. As we were getting ready to hit the house with a search warrant, the news people showed up with cameras. Denny told one of them, "If you turn the strobe lights on, I will deck you!" Of course, the concern was that lighting us up might get us killed if Kessler was in the house. The cameraman was not overly bright, and he got knocked on his ass.

After we gained entry, Bob Peterson and I searched the house. We were looking for Kessler and any evidence that might be helpful. In searching, Bob found an Oregonian newspaper article with our names and photos from a previous case that he and I had worked on. There was a red circle around the article and our photos. That was interesting, to say the least.

Denny Branagan would have been a good poster boy for the Marines. He was built like a tank. He was also one of the nicest people I have ever known, but he didn't take shit from anyone. This incident was on the weekend. Denny had to be in a staff meeting the following Monday. Sheriff Fred Pearce told Denny that he had heard that there was a problem with the press over the weekend. Denny quickly confessed, only to find out that Fred Pearce totally approved of his actions.

MY CHASE WITH THE F.B.I.

Kessler was unaware of how much we knew about his operation. Some of his associates continued dealing heroin to Bobbie and me, so we knew our cover was still intact. One particular "buy" was set up between Richard Ruip and Bobbie. He was the same person we were buying from when Kessler shot at police and fled into the woods earlier. Bobbie bought an ounce of heroin from Ruip. After the deal was done, a signal was broadcast that Ruip needed to be arrested.

As he headed East into the Parkrose area of Portland, he sensed that we were behind him. We had called for a uniform car to assist with a felony stop, but that car was not with us yet. I was in the area in an old, beater Chevy with a big engine. Stan "the man" Renning from the F.B.I. was my partner at the moment, and the chase was on. Ruip was driving a fast car, but he lost control of his car at 99th and NE Sandy Blvd. and rear-ended a small compact pickup that was stopped at a light. I saw the rear window of the pickup smash, and at the same time, I witnessed our tracking device fly away at about sixty m.p.h. from underneath Ruip's car.

The tracker had really become a missile at that point, as it was a heavy device full of D cell batteries.

As if this were not enough, the situation continued to escalate. Ruip had an extensive criminal record and realized that he would be in a world of hurt if caught. He spontaneously decided to throw out our $7,000 in marked "buy" money. It was breezy that afternoon, and I could still see our carefully procured dollars fluttering in the wind. By this time, we had ample law enforcement on the scene, and Ruip was quickly taken into custody. Richard Ruip, who had narrowly escaped my grasp before, went away for a number of years after this escapade.

United States Department of Justice

UNITED STATES ATTORNEY
District of Oregon
312 United States Courthouse
620 S.W. Main
PORTLAND, OREGON 97205

(503) 221-2101

April 30, 1982

15:cas

Special Agent E. Neil Van Horn
Drug Enforcement Administration
1220 S. W. Morrison, Room 706
Portland, Oregon 97205

Detective Robert J. Peterson
City of Gresham
Department of Police
1333 N.W. Eastman
Gresham, Oregon 97030

Sergeant Bill Goss
Multnomah County Division of Public Safety
12240 N. E. Glisan
Portland, Oregon 97230

Deputy Chris Peterson
Multnomah County Division of Public Safety
12240 N. E. Glisan
Portland, Oregon 97230

Deputy Mike Unsworth
Multnomah County Division of Public Safety
12240 N. E. Glisan
Portland, Oregon 97205

Deputy Lee Houston
Multnomah County Division of Public Safety
12240 N. E. Glisan
Portland, Oregon 97230

Deputy Herschel Lange
Multnomah County Division of Public Safety
12240 N. E. Glisan
Portland, Oregon 97230

Re: United States v. Richard Charles Ruip
No. CR 82-25-1(PA)

Gentlemen:

As I am sure all of you know by now, the jury convicted Mr. Ruip of both counts on April 29, 1982, at approximately 4:00 p.m. Count I charged him with conspiracy to distribute heroin and Count II charged him with distribution of heroin. Judge Panner will impose sentence on June 7, 1982, probably in the morning.

The maximum penalty that could be imposed upon Mr. Ruip is 30 years in prison, a $50,000 fine and life on special parole. I myself am hoping that Mr. Ruip receives a sentence of between 20-25 years and life on special parole. In view of his previous convictions, perhaps we can keep him in jail until he is eligible for social security.

I wanted to thank each and every one of you for your aid in helping me prepare for trial. I personally want to commend the Peterson brothers, Chris and Bob, for their work in making the case against Mr. Ruip. It is my opinion

Letter of commendation for the Peterson "Brothers" help in the federal dope case of Richard Ruip from Charles Turner, Oregon US Attorney (1)

129

that these two officers helped remove a very dangerous person from the streets.

As you know, after a lengthy record in the 1950's, Mr. Ruip was arrested for a bank robbery on May 9, 1961, and was subsequently sentenced to 15 years in federal prison. He was released on October 1, 1969, by federal authorities to the State of Ohio authorities. He was subsequently released by the State of Ohio on June 17, 1970. By April 6, 1971, or a mere 10 months later, Mr. Ruip was involved in another armed bank robbery and shootout with police as his accomplices left the bank. While in jail and after having been sentenced to 18 years for this bank robbery, that being on August 8, 1971, he and his present wife attempted his escape from prison. He was released from federal prison on these last convictions on November 16, 1979, and became a Portland resident in August, 1980. He was, of course, arrested on these charges on February 17, 1982, so basically what you have in the case of Mr. Ruip is a person who has only been on the street for about 37 months in the last 21 years.

Since we in the federal government put him on the street, it is our responsibility to take him back off, and with Chris and Bob's help, we have done so. Thank you all very much.

Yours truly,

CHARLES H. TURNER
United States Attorney

KENNETH C. BAUMAN
Assistant United States Attorney

Letter of commendation for the Peterson "Brothers" help in the federal dope case of Richard Ruip from Charles Turner, Oregon US Attorney (2)

ARMED ROBBERY AT THE FLAMINGO

Just about this time, the tone alert on my radio went off, and the dispatcher said there was an armed robbery at the Flamingo Motel. I thought that was really convenient, as I was only one hundred yards from that location. Deputy Ard Pratt and I ran towards to motel office. Ard was in uniform, but I went through the office door first. In retrospect, that was a mistake. Ard was a few steps behind me. I saw two or three people duck under the counter and then disappear from sight. There was little doubt in my mind that we had a hostage situation. As it turned out, there was a stairway to the basement of the motel. Ard and I raced down the stairs looking for the kidnapper. As I rounded one corner and burst into the room with my gun in hand, I said something like, "Freeze, you blankety-blank." I found myself looking at the Parkrose Rotary Club having a monthly meeting. Needless to say, they were as surprised by this situation as I was.

The motel clerks had seen our recent activity nearby in the middle of the street. They saw a lot of guns being waved around, and of course, there were no marked police cars visible as we initially tried to arrest Ruip. The clerks had reported the so-called "robbery," and evidently, we were the perpetrators. Such is the life of an undercover police officer.

LUCKY WOMAN WITH TWO MEN

We continued buying dope from Valerie and Tammy, and they kept cashing our traveler's checks. They had unwittingly been our introduction into the Kessler crew. Even though they were low-level players in this crowd, we still had to arrest them. During one purchase of heroin, Valerie said she had been told to check me for a body wire. I was, in fact, wearing one at the time, but she got sidetracked for a moment. I quickly went into the bathroom of her home and put the wire into the toilet tank. I then made the buy. Bob Peterson and John Bunnell were nearby monitoring the entire situation, and I was able to let them know that I was taking the wire off.

A day or two later, we arrested both of the ladies. They were cooperative, and we gathered as much information as we could from them. By the time Bobbie and I were done talking to Valerie, it was getting late in the evening. We headed towards downtown Portland to book her into jail. We actually really liked both of the ladies, so this arrest was bittersweet. Valerie said she was hungry and asked if we could get her something to eat before going to jail. We knew that the jail would not feed her at that time of night. There were no convenient restaurants nearby, but the Hilton Hotel was open and had a nice dining room on the top floor. We took Valerie's handcuffs off and proceeded to the lobby's elevator. As the elevator door opened, an intoxicated woman stepped off. She saw Valerie standing there with the two of us and said, "Oh, you lucky girl with two men." We all got a chuckle out of that one, and Valerie went to jail on a full stomach.

As I was working on this book, I reached out to Bobbie Peterson on New Year's Day of 2021 and asked him what he thought were the three most interesting cases we had while working together. His immediate answer the next day was, "Top of my list is the Kessler group. Bobbie then went on to mention the five persons associated with Kessler that we had arrested, and Valerie was one of them. Another person Bobbie mentioned was Sheri Resner, who lived at 53 SE 84th Ave. in Portland. This was the house where Bobbie and I saw a newspaper article with our photos circled in red. We didn't arrest Sheri.

MAJOR DOPE DEALER

One day I was sitting in our undercover floating home. We looked like the playboys of the year. The home was near Jantzen Beach on the Columbia River. We had a ski boat, a lot of flashy cars, and access to large amounts of "buy money." The phone rang, and I answered it. I recognized the caller as Marc Gaudry by his voice. Marc asked to speak with John, so I handed the phone to him. John had been working with Marc in an attempt to put a large cocaine deal together. John did not know who Marc was, and clearly, Marc did not know that the John he was speaking to was none other than John Bunnell: leader of the county dope unit.

Multnomah County and Washington County Dope Units - 1980s.

The reason that I recognized Marc's voice was that he and his brother owned a lively bar at 102nd and NE Halsey called The Keyhole. This club was in my district, and I frequented the place. Marc's brother was one of my best friends; we were fishing and camping pals. I had gotten to know Marc as well. I had been to his home and met his wife. We were certainly acquaintances. I had noticed that Marc's standard of living seemed to be higher than that of his brother, but I had no idea that he was a significant player in the Portland cocaine trade.

Bunnell and Marc worked out the dope deal. I was not involved at this time. The day arrived for the deal to go down, and the location for the meet was at the Holiday Inn in Wilsonville, OR. We had the place surrounded by dope cops and had rented the room next door to where the money and dope were to be exchanged. Since we knew who we were dealing with, Marc showed up and was quickly arrested without incident. We seized a significant amount of cocaine. To say that Marc was surprised to see me there would be a bit of an understatement.

When working big dope cases, it was never advisable to put players like Marc in jail immediately if you thought they could lead you to the proverbial "big fish." In short, smaller fish are used as bait to hook larger fish. It is better to get these lower-level dealers to cooperate and trace sales up the food chain to the larger distributors. News of dope arrests always spreads quickly in the underworld. If a dealer has been arrested, they are soon not trusted by others in the business, as everyone understands the "big fish" theory.

John and Marc made an agreement: he would turn over his connection in exchange for a break on the charges. Marc and I spent a night at the hotel in anticipation of working on the "big fish." The next morning Marc and I said goodbye for the moment as he and John were finalizing the agreement. This situation didn't quite work out, though, as

135

Marc quickly fled the country for Puerto Vallarta, Mexico, where his parents had a second home. We couldn't get Marc extradited from Mexico because he was actually a Canadian citizen. Marc most likely got back into the business, as one of his brothers was later killed by the police in Mexico. Shortly after the Gaudry investigation, I was again rotated back into uniform patrol. Arresting Marc Gaudry was difficult for me. We had been friends in a minor way. I had met his family, including his dad, and was best friends with his brother. It was good police work, though, and an example of how getting out and mixing with the public could be beneficial to the taxpayers.

Before I retired, I attended a language school in Puerto Vallarta, Mexico in 1994. The county had actually sent me to a Spanish school in Cuernavaca, Mexico, several years earlier. After school in Puerto Vallarta, I started visiting this Mexican town regularly. I was staying in a small condo complex called Ibiza. The guy who owned the penthouse was named Steve Stone, and he was a flashy, obnoxious individual. Steve ran a timeshare property business; he was abusive to his wife and treated other owners in the complex poorly. It soon became apparent to me that Steve was also in the dope business. He had all kinds of security concerns, and I noticed questionable people coming and going from his place. This, however, was not my concern, as I was in a foreign country and knew that my value as a cop from the U.S. meant nothing down there.

I had heard that Marc Gaudry was in Puerto Vallarta selling timeshares and that he had married the local police chief's daughter. I also learned that Steve Stone's boss in the timeshare business was an American named Marc. That tidbit of information gave me some pause, to be sure. Steve Stone had a cat that was in heat. He would put it outside his unit because it was keeping his wife awake, yowling. During one of my visits there, it kept the whole place awake. The next day I talked to the groundskeeper or "mozo" and asked him, half joking, how much it would cost to get a cat killed in Mexico. This information was quickly relayed to Steve, and he left a note on my condo door advising me never to rent in that complex again.

In retrospect, I thought that Steve probably worked for Marc Gaudry in the timeshare business. Marc knew my role in his capture back in the states and had fled the U.S. I now had a similar conflict with a dope dealer in Mexico. I was irritated to no end about Steve telling me that I wasn't welcome in the complex. Living in the penthouse, Steve had to come down a spiral staircase to go to work. The day after the threat, I went and sat in a chair at the bottom of the stairs. When Steve came down, I was essentially blocking his exit.

I asked him if there was something he wished to speak with me about, but he declined my offer for a discussion.

There was a hotel just West of Ibiza known as the Hotel La Siesta. Several years after my interaction with Steve, he was spun out on drugs and jumped off of the top of this high-rise hotel. After this, Steve was no longer a problem to me or the world at large. Years later, I had an occasion to speak with Marc Gaudry, who was now living in a different part of Mexico. He was still selling timeshares. I asked him if he knew Steve, and he said he didn't. Who really knows what the truth of this situation is? Marc still can't come back to the U.S., though, as he has an outstanding warrant. So much for Marc and Steve.

Chapter 10

UNIFORM: 1984

At one time, the U.S. Attorney for the District of Oregon was Charles Turner; I like to call him "Charlie." We got to know Charlie well, as a lot of our significant narcotics cases were tried in federal court. One afternoon a bunch of us had stopped for a drink at the Flower Drum bar on 145th and SE Division St. in Portland. Charlie called Bob Peterson to tell him that someone had kidnapped his secretary's dog and was holding it for ransom. He asked if we could assist her. We found out how much money the ransom demand was but didn't have enough to cover that amount. The owner of the club, Uncle Ray, was sitting at the table with us. He went to the till and got the needed $100 ransom.

We lured the dog napper to the "Drum" parking lot, and sure enough, he showed up with the animal. Uncle Ray was with me in my car, waiting for the suspect to arrive. There were also four or five other police officers involved. One of us showed the thief the money, got the dog back, and didn't arrest him. When I jumped out of my undercover car, I forgot to put it in park, so it rolled towards the suspect's auto with Uncle Ray sitting on the passenger side desperately trying to get to the brake. Ultimately, he got it stopped. We eventually turned the suspect loose and gave Uncle Ray his money back. Ray was laughing and shaking his head, saying, "That Charlie Turner must be a really important guy." The "Drum" was not really a cop hangout. It was a lively country western bar, and one of the owners was one of my best friends. Uncle Ray liked us, cops.

THE YOUNG SISTERS

There was a pair of drop-dead gorgeous sisters who sang at the "Drum" for years. Their mother waitressed at the bar. One day, while on Routine Patrol, I saw one of the young sisters walking near her apartment. It was broad daylight in a busy part of town, and she asked me if I would give her a ride to the store which was nearby. I said sure but told her she would have to sit in the back seat, as I had briefcases and shotguns in front. She happily jumped into the back seat, and we headed for the store. I noticed all the nearby drivers were paying a lot of attention to the right side of my car. I couldn't figure it out until I glanced in my rearview mirror and saw my passenger with two bare breasts plastered against the window. I am glad we were able to provide some entertainment on that sunny summer afternoon.

This was another example of a naked woman entertaining the public from the back seat of my police car.

SPLIT SECOND DECISION

In 1984, my son Tod was stationed at a naval air base in Maine. I made plans to go visit him and worked my regular shift the night before leaving on the trip. I had an unusual conversation with myself before I went to work that day. I thought, "Don't let anything bad happen before you get on that plane." I was clearly missing my son and did not want anything to interfere with my trip to see him.

I had a trainee recruit riding with me that night. We received a call to go to an area of small cabins on SE 136th. I was quite familiar with these cabins, which were used to house migrant farm workers. As I was working on my Spanish, I would stop there on a regular basis to practice speaking with the young kids before spoiling them with candy. The call was regarding gunshots in the area. This did not alarm me, as the occupants of the cabins were always shooting off fireworks.

I pulled into the complex with my side of the car closest to the cabins. As usual, the police car was immediately surrounded by my little Mexican buddies looking for their sugar fix. My recruit was sitting on the passenger side of the car, so he could not see the terrifying situation that unfolded mere moments later. I looked out of the car window to my left and saw an open cabin door with a Mexican male brandishing a gun in my general direction. I had no idea what his intentions were and couldn't hit the gas to move backward or forwards because my little friends were all around me. I had no time to discuss the situation with my recruit.

This was one of those impossible situations that police officers encounter regularly. Of course, juries and judges can ponder these scenarios for days after the fact, but I did not have that kind of time. There were no good options for me. In a millisecond, I decided to jump out of the car and charge. The man was twenty feet away and two to three steps above me as he stood at the cabin door. Charging the gunman was not what any police tactical instructor would have recommended. I had my .357 revolver in hand and was three feet away from the man, telling him in my beginner Spanish to drop his weapon. As I stared at the white walls behind him, I thought about what they would look like if I pulled the trigger. I guess my luck held, and my Spanish was adequate, as the man dropped his gun.

Had I been killed, there would have been the usual news coverage and grieving. My friends would have worn black bands over their badges for a few days. Had I killed the man, there would have been concerns about my conduct and an officer-involved shooting investigation. If that happened today, there would have been cries of police brutality against those folks with darker skin. I was lucky that August day in 1982, and so was the man in the cabin.

MT. HOOD SECURITY BANK ROBBERY: BULLETS FLYING/ GUS TURNER

On September 2, 1984, I had one of those experiences that no cop wants to have. At this point, I was halfway through my career with the Multnomah County Sheriff's Office. By this time, I had a lot of experience with crime and violent offenders. I was on Routine Patrol, or R.P. when a rarely used tone alert came over the radio that grabbed my immediate attention. The tone alert was used by the communications center when a vitally significant message needed to get out to all the officers. It was used infrequently and normally only in dire circumstances.

This was in the early afternoon on a warm day. The Mt. Hood Security Bank in Gresham, OR, had just been robbed, and one of my colleagues, Jerry Pritchard, was in his patrol car pursuing the bank robber. Jerry had a new recruit with him, and as the chase progressed, the robber started shooting at his car. One of the rounds ricocheted off the pavement and came up through the floorboard of Jerry's car. He was hit in the leg, and his pursuit was soon over. We had a description of the robber's car, which was soon located nearby, but the perpetrator had abandoned it. A witness thought that the driver had gotten into a van, and a description of the new vehicle was put out over the radio.

The Gresham area was soon swarming with police vehicles from a number of agencies as well as the F.B.I. Bank Robbery Squad. Several hours after the shooting, Multnomah County Deputy Steve Crampton observed the possible suspect van parked in a trailer court in the nearby neighborhood of Wood Village. Four more Multnomah Deputies arrived, and as we were moving rapidly on foot towards the van, we were suddenly being shot at with an AR-15 assault rifle. Miraculously, none of us were hit.

The shooter was then seen breaking into the door of a mobile home with the butt of his AR-15, and he was soon out of sight. This is how the standoff started. I was positioned to the north of the trailer, and standing by my side was Stan Renning, one of the great F.B.I. bank robbery experts in the country. I had become close to Stan during the Kessler/Ruip investigations. Stan was a fearless guy. He said, "Do you know who this is? It is Gus Turner." I probably had my doubts about that but wisely chose not to voice them to "Stan the man."

The standoff continued for several hours. We were throwing smoke grenades through the window, and soon the trailer was full of smoke and smoldering. This went on for

144

some time, and I thought no one could survive the lack of oxygen. As it turned out, Gus Turner was the bad guy. He had managed to dig through the floor of the trailer, which was about to burst into flames and was now underneath it. The Portland Police S.W.A.T. team arrived, and a semi-conscious Turner was ultimately dragged out from under the trailer and taken by ambulance to the hospital.

Although I worked in Portland, I was living in Vancouver, WA, and therefore paid a lot of attention to crime in both areas. On August 16, 1984, just two weeks prior to the Gus Turner incident, a woman was robbed while getting out of her car to go work at the Safe Credit Union at the 2700 block of Evergreen Blvd. in Vancouver, WA. As she was preparing to get out of her car, the woman saw a menacing-looking man approach. She stayed in her car for a few minutes until the man was no longer in sight. When she finally got out, the man reappeared and ordered her to get back into her car.

The woman ran, throwing her purse into the middle of the street, thinking that was what the man wanted. The man fired a shot into the ground, grabbed the purse, and took off running. The woman screamed, and about this time, a civilian named Richard Martens was approaching on his motorcycle. He stopped to see what the problem was, and the woman told him what had happened. Martens quickly caught up with the suspect near an apartment complex. The man turned and shot Martens in the chest with a .38 revolver, and he died shortly after 9:00 a.m. that morning. Vancouver Police Chief Leland Davis posthumously awarded a commendation to Richard Marten's family for his bravery.

Police swarmed the area but were unable to locate the shooter, who was described as a white male, five feet and six inches tall, twenty to thirty years old, with brown curly hair and a slight build. The man was not located that day, but he was found several weeks later.

A month earlier, on August 5, 1984, convicted bank robber Gus Turner had escaped from the Lewis County, WA Jail. Between his escape and September 2 of that same year, he committed several more credit union and bank robberies. Turner was sentenced to life in prison and is incarcerated in Walla Walla, WA.

JUMPING OUT THE WINDOW

Having previously been assigned to a burglary task force, I had become adept at working these cases. I got to know a lot of professional burglars. Some were not great at their work, and others were actually pretty good at it. One that wasn't so great was Steve Truax. Steve was a skinny little character, and his burglary career was based on his need for drugs. I had arrested Steve a number of times, and we sort of had a "professional relationship." There were never any harsh words between us, and Steve was never snarky with me.

On January 4, 1984, I got a call for a burglary at 14046 SE Ellis St. in Portland. After hearing about the M.O. and the description of the burglar, I suspected that the culprit was likely Truax. I knew where Steve was living, so I went looking for him at his two-story home on SE 136th Ave. overlooking the railroad tracks. After some gentle persuasion, Steve finally confessed and was arrested.

Steve told me that he needed to take a shit knowing that I would suspect he was telling the truth and did not want him messing up the back of my police car. I knew that the bathroom was ten to twelve feet off the ground, so I didn't think Steve would want to jump out the window. I checked the bathroom for firearms and then told him to make it quick. Moments later, I heard the wood-framed window in the bathroom being opened. I kicked down the locked door only to find the room empty. Steve had jumped out! Yes, this was professionally embarrassing, but it also pissed me off. My little buddy Steve Truax got me. I called for cover cars to assist me in looking for him, so I had lots of help trying to find my "mistake."

I was never interested in being a canine handler but always appreciated the dogs and their abilities to find folks. On this particular night, Steve Smith showed up to assist. His dog was a big shepherd. At one point, I looked out of the second-story window to see Smith and his dog engaged in a struggle with each other, and I wasn't sure who was winning. I found out that the struggle was all about who the alpha male was and that these struggles were not totally uncommon while working with strong-willed dogs. It was amusing to watch as I thought about my little buddy Steve Truax quickly making his getaway.

Due to my many varied assignments, I had an incredible group of snitches. I would like to think that this was the case because I tended to treat bad guys well. The word was that I was looking for Truax. I soon had the address of a house in nearby Milwaukie, OR, where he was hiding. I reached out to Ray Burgarsky, a career deputy with the M.C.S.O. and a great cop. Ray said he would be happy to assist, so away we went to Milwaukie in two marked police cars. I drove by the house after dark and saw Steve inside. He moved quickly out of sight as Ray and I jumped out and hit the house. There were several guys inside, and I was trying to maintain some order while Ray looked for Steve. Ray finally found him hiding under a bed. I heard "pleasantries" exchanged, and soon Steve was in handcuffs with a new charge of escape added to his original burglary charge.

Chapter 11

NIGHT DETECTIVES: 1985-1990 BRANAGAN & PETERSON

One of the best assignments I had at the sheriff's office was working as a night detective. This was a good time of day to be at work, as all the bosses were gone. The building was quiet, and we pretty much had the whole place to ourselves. My partner working this shift was Denny Branagan. We had a lot of memorable cases during these days. Those two and a half years were probably the most interesting times in my police career. Denny had a comfortable home and acreage in Gresham, OR, where our beat was. We would stop by his house occasionally, and his lovely wife Mary would prepare us meals. I also got to know his two daughters; they were all like family.

Night Detectives Dennis Branagan and Chris Peterson – working on a case in Los Angeles

When one spends ten hours a day, forty-plus hours a week together, often in stressful situations, a serious bond, that only a few people understand, develops. There weren't many folks I knew as well as I knew Denny. There are few secrets in this kind of relationship. Our politics were similar, our desire to make Portland a better place was the same, and we were paid well enough to feel as if we should earn that pay.

We were both veterans, which was a common bond. Denny was a former marine and was quite proud of his service. He always told me when it was the marine corps' birthday. During the mid-80s, there was a movement in the U.S. Military allowing standards in appearance to change. Military folks were allowed to wear their hair longer and grow beards or mustaches. Denny felt that this change was not positive, and he wrote a letter to the Commandant of the Marine Corp, General Gray. He got a written reply from General Gray thanking him for his opinion on the issue. I suspect this letter was one of Denny's prized possessions.

While he was overseas in the marine corps, Denny's father, who was a sports reporter for *The Oregonian*, died suddenly of a heart attack. This event had a huge impact on the rest of his life. He would do occasional custom farm work; he loved to be outdoors and enjoyed riding his tractor. I never really appreciated that type of work until years later. After retiring, I purchased a Kubota Tractor that I named K.T. and some acreage of land, which became the Lazy J. This was my grandfather's brand, and it is still used by the family in Idaho. I occasionally would tell my wife that I needed to spend therapy time with Dr. Kubota and would then go to work on the land.

DECAPITATED

One of the more memorable cases Denny and I worked on was in March of 1986 when Daniel William Pierce disappeared from his home on SW 23rd Cir. in Troutdale, OR. Daniel had two or three roommates, and one of them was a female who waitressed at a local restaurant. The woman expressed her concerns to a local police officer who frequented her place of employment. She had nothing firm other than the fact that her roommate had not come home for a few days.

Ultimately, Denny and I went to the house with our team of crime scene investigators. They identified blood in the missing person's bedroom, and it was apparent that efforts had been made to clean up a crime scene. This evidence prompted us to start a serious investigation. As we searched the house, it became apparent that a third roommate was no longer around. We discovered that this roommate, the second one to disappear, including Daniel, had an interesting past. Initially, we were not certain of his identity but thought he was Socrates Ladner, A.K.A. Dan Brown.

We found a lot of paperwork in the house that showed he was a very clever man who had learned how to develop aliases that were amazingly good. He would put an ad in newspapers around the country seeking an employee to manage a small pizza business. The suggested salary would be attractive. He would ask for resumes to be sent to a P.O. Box, and they would pour in by the dozens. He could then use the information provided on each resume to assume the identity of the applicant. At the outset of the investigation, we examined a stack of resumes. The applicants would provide their full name, social security number, and date of birth. In this manner, Socrates had a new identification whenever he needed one. Although he had a number of aliases, Socrates Ladner was the name we went with. We discovered that he likely came from Panama and had left a trail of crime around that country as well.

Socrates had come to the Portland area from Seattle. He was a handsome young man who had been telling people in Seattle that he was a Boeing engineer. He moved into a home with multiple roommates and was living there as the "engineer." When he decided to leave Seattle for reasons unknown, he cleaned out any valuables that his roommates had on his way out of town. He then promptly went to a local car dealership and drove away with a brand-new stolen car.

Socrates was currently working at a pizza place in East Portland, and he was still driving the stolen car. The roommate that was initially missing, Daniel Pierce, must have learned about Socrates' past and likely discovered some ongoing crimes which ultimately resulted in his death.

It is believed that he was murdered in his bed and then beheaded. We speculated that Socrates removed the victim's head in the hopes of slowing the discovery of Daniel's identity since dental records were often used to determine such information. During this investigation, we learned that Ladner had an elderly grandmother visiting from Panama, which no doubt interfered with his plans to flee town.

Denny and I were told by our Lt. to watch a suspect house in case Ladner showed up. We talked about the Lt.'s idea and thought of a way better plan. We knew that Ladner had a dog and thought that he had likely left the animal with someone he knew. This person lived in a trailer park on SE Division St. in Portland. We knew that he would likely go get his dog before leaving the Portland area. We set up a surveillance and then sat in our economical K car at the trailer park where we thought the dog might be. As the night wore on, we saw no sign of our killer and started getting anxious. If our hunch that he was coming to this location was wrong, it would piss off the Lt. to no end. About midnight, we saw a small U-Haul truck slip quietly into the trailer park with its headlights out and only one person in the front cab. With smiles on our faces, Denny and I quietly got out of the car and accosted Ladner. After a short struggle, he was in custody. We interviewed Ladner until the wee hours of the morning but obtained no helpful statements from him. Denny and I had developed a bond that was remarkable. We could read each other's minds. We were involved in a number of harrowing and difficult situations together. We never had a disagreement or unpleasant interaction with each other.

Other detectives involved in the surveillance of Ladner located his grandmother and the stolen car he had been driving at a motel in Lake Oswego, OR. The grandmother was contacted, the stolen car was towed, and a search warrant was obtained for it. The victim's severed head was located in the trunk of the car early the next day after we arrested Ladner. We told him about the grandmother, hotel, car, and severed head, and he knew that his days as a free man were over. Ladner quickly entered a guilty plea to the murder before the D.A.'s office had even received a single written report regarding his arrest. He had outstanding warrants from Texas for escape and parole violations when we arrested him. In homicide cases, a murder book is created for each crime, and we started ours on this case that very day. Sometimes this book is several loose-leaf binders; other times, it is longer. No matter how thick the murder book is, there are lots of reports to be written before a case goes to a trial or a plea is entered. We had our work cut out for us on the Ladner case.

MY F.B.I. "FRIENDS"

We got a call one night from my friend, Mike McGettigan, who owned a shop called Stereo Super Stores. He would call me occasionally with concerns because he knew I would take them seriously. After all, I was getting paid to investigate crimes. Mike told me his stereo warehouse on NW Yeon St. in Portland had been burglarized, and a diesel truck with $250,000 worth of merchandise had been stolen. I knew the warehouse was in the City of Portland, and I told Mike that crossing those jurisdictional lines could create problems for me. He said he could care less about that issue, as his security director had contacted the Portland Police and the F.B.I. to no avail.

I said to myself, "Here we go again!" I called the P.P.D. Detective's Office and was told that Det. Pat McGuire was investigating this burglary. Pat was a great cop and a good friend, but he was out of town. Mike's security director was Tim Debauw, a former Multnomah County Deputy. Tim had done some work on the case and learned the name of a person who had likely fenced the stolen goods. After getting the name of the fence, we went to a nasty bar located in downtown Vancouver, WA, where he was working as a bartender.

We walked into the bar in our casual clothing, cowboy boots, and Levi's and ordered soft drinks. This was a clear message to the bartender, who likely had a criminal background, that something was off; why are these guys not drinking in a bar? We were fairly young and healthy looking, which was also out of place in this nasty joint. We sat at a table for twenty minutes or so, hoping to see something interesting, but nothing popped up. It got really slow in the bar, so we moved forward and had a private chat with the bartender and alleged fence. The man informed us that he was on parole and had a terminal case of lung cancer. We learned enough about the stolen items that we could probably have arrested him, but he wasn't who we really wanted.

He gave us an address in Clackamas County where we believed some of the stolen stereo goods might be. He also told us where we could find the stolen truck from the burglary. We went to a truck stop in Troutdale, OR, and recovered the stolen vehicle. After it was processed for evidence and prints, the truck was then cleared out of the national computer (N.C.I.C.) as a stolen vehicle.

During this early investigation, I got a call from a young female F.B.I. agent named Karen, who was very demanding and wanted to know what we were doing investigating this burglary. She had been assigned to the stereo case but did not have a clue what to do with it. She was new to her job, and the case was likely dumped on her. Agent Karen irritated me with her approach, so I told her the case was "Crypto Top Secret." This was my way of trying to tell her to butt out. Karen hung up the phone and told her boss about the "Crypto Top Secret" status of the case. Shortly thereafter, I got a call from her F.B.I. supervisor; we'll call him Charlie. Charlie started reading me the riot act for several minutes. When I thought he was starting to get hoarse, I said, "Charlie, go "----" yourself." Keep in mind, at this point in time, we had not recovered any stolen property except the truck. The call ended rather abruptly, and I got back to doing what needed to be done to solve this case.

Being a small agency, Denny and I were close to all the dope cops. The county dope unit was across the hall from the night detective's office. We needed some surveillance help. We couldn't do this task alone. I contacted Bob "Bobbie" Peterson, who was on loan to the county from the Gresham Police Department. I contacted Eddie Fisher as well; he was also assigned to the dope unit. Eddie was a Federal Immigration Officer, and he was renowned for his work ethic.

Bobbie, Eddie, Denny, myself, and several others got down to work. We set up surveillance on the house in Clackamas County and soon identified a suspect car. We followed it to a commercial storage locker several miles away and determined which locker the car went to. After the unidentified crook left the storage locker, we followed the car and made a traffic stop several miles away. The driver was identified as Joe Siebold. Sure enough, he had a trunk full of stolen property from the stereo store. We subsequently learned that this group of criminals were some of the most professional burglars in the entire city. When I say the term "professional burglar," I simply mean that these criminals were very good at stealing and weren't just committing crimes to feed their drug habit. A search warrant on the locker revealed half of the stolen property. We called Mike McGettigan and told him to send a truck to haul the recovered property away.

About three that morning, we were done, and I called Mike at his house, telling him to get the cocktails ready because we were coming by to celebrate. Mike and his girlfriend Sherry had a beautiful floating home on the Columbia River. They got out of bed, and the celebration started. Ironically Mike, Sherry, and I remain best friends to this day despite the fact that we woke them in the middle of the night and made them party with us after the case was solved. They had a beautiful yacht, the Ambar, in LaPaz, Mexico, on the Sea of Cortez. Mike has spent many years trying to save this beautiful body of water from a multitude of threats. My family was treated to several cruises in the

Sea of Cortez aboard the Ambar. This started my love for the country of Mexico and led me to learn the language, which I still work on.

After the storage unit arrest and recovery, we learned one of the other suspects was named Willie, and he lived in a flop house hotel in SW Portland. I knew the nice lady who managed the hotel. We paid her a visit, and she gave us lots of intel about Willie. At this point, I learned that much of the stolen property may have gone to Seattle. There was little doubt that Willie would be the key to recovering that property. We now knew what kind of car Willie drove and where he parked it at the hotel.

Since the property had likely left the state of Oregon, I thought that this would be a good time to involve the F.B.I. That fact was kind of a given at this point. They could run a lot farther than we could with this good intel. I called Karen and told her that I might be able to help her with her F.B.I. case on these burglars. She seemed happy to hear this but said not to tell her boss Charlie that she was talking to me. Karen came to the hotel and met with us "locals" as the F.B.I. called us. We handed the case to her on a silver platter and let her get to work. Several months later, the hotel manager called me with a request for some police assistance. I asked her what had happened with Willie and the F.B.I. She said that agents came by the next day and spoke with Willie, and he was never seen again. Of course, no one was arrested, and no property was recovered. This was often the case when the F.B.I. got involved in local criminal investigations.

When the F.B.I. was formed, police corruption was at an all-time high. This was particularly true on the East Coast and some of the big Midwestern cities. The F.B.I. was formed in response to those problems, and this fact clouded issues between the federal agents and the local police departments for many years. The F.B.I. didn't trust the locals, and the locals didn't like the F.B.I. because they would not share information. I think that this was still a problem early in my career. Ironically, I became fast friends with many of the Portland F.B.I. agents years later. I am still close with many of these officers years after retiring from law enforcement. The fact that local departments and the F.B.I. joined ranks in many task forces over the years eroded lots of these issues that had existed for some time.

LARCH MOUNTAIN DOUBLE MURDER

On December 30, 1987, Denny and I got a call about a murder on Larch Mountain near Corbett. The remoteness of this area attracted problems from the nearby urban neighborhoods in Portland. Larch Mountain was where a bunch of bodies were dumped, and a significant number of murders were committed over the years. We arrived and got briefed by the uniformed officers on the scene. What we knew initially was that a dead body was found in a car that had been set on fire. There was another victim who had been shot and set on fire but managed to escape the car and roll in several inches of the snow that covered the ground. The survivor, John Rodger Elmer, was badly burned and was flown to the trauma unit at Emanuel Hospital in Portland.

We decided to split up. Denny stayed at the crime scene, and I went to the Emanuel Burn Center. Upon arrival, I was allowed to interview the victim, who was barely coherent. It quickly became apparent that this case would have a number of challenges. The patient was a convict, and he clearly did not want to be my friend. He was willing to tell me the name of the other victim, but that was about the extent of his statements initially. The deceased person was forty-nine years old; his name was John Leslie Beach.

John Elmer said he had been sitting in the car when the assailant shot through the closed car window shattering the glass and spraying fragments into his eyes. Someone then opened the car door, poured gas into the interior, and set it on fire. It was determined at the autopsy that Beach had been shot, killed, and then set on fire. The location of this assault was remote; there were no witnesses, no cameras, and no obvious evidence left at the scene.

Denny had remained at the crime scene. After several long hours, I talked to him and asked what was taking him so long to get to my location. He patiently explained that they had decided to tow the deceased victim and the car to a secure spot where a medical examiner would have better conditions to conduct an analysis of the crime scene, body, and car. When we arrived, the victim and car were still smoldering. Corbett volunteer firefighters had put out the fire, but the victim's body reignited as the car was being prepared for towing. Denny had to call the firefighters back to the car to put the fire out once again. After this incident, the victim's body was burned beyond recognition.

A common denominator among the criminal element was what cops liked to call their "asshole book." This was a small address book that seemed to be a requirement for any serious felon. John Beach's book had been in his jeans back pocket, and he was sitting on it when he died. The book, which reeked of gasoline, survived, and it held many of the keys we needed for a successful prosecution. For you younger readers, this was before the days of the smartphone that now holds everyone's contacts, although police use these newer electronic devices in much the same manner today. We spent many hours examining the "asshole book." It was sort of a who's who of bad guys in Oregon and Washington. One of the names in the book was a murderer who had kidnapped and killed a young woman while she was jogging late at night in Vancouver, WA's Cascade Park.

Meanwhile, the other victim, John Elmer, was still suffering from severe wounds in the burn center. We spent countless frustrating days and hours trying to interview him. Slowly, he finally started to cooperate. We learned that he and John Beach had been locked up together in the State Penitentiary in Shelton, WA. Beach had recently escaped from this fine establishment where he had become acquainted with John Elmer, Phil Gurule, and Steve Shelton. One of the Larch Mt. killers was Phil Gurule, and the other was Steve Shelton. The victim who lived, John Elmer, had never gotten out of his "con" mentality, but he slowly provided details that helped us locate and arrest both suspects.

HITS HIRED ON BRANAGAN, PETERSON, AND HARDMAN

Phil Gurule and Steve Shelton were finally in the Multnomah County Jail awaiting trial for murder and assault. The DAs assigned to the case were Chris Hardman and Michael Brown. Denny and I never had a close relationship with Hardman, but we were moving ahead for a trial. As we were preparing for the trial, we learned that the suspects were recruiting someone to kill Denny, myself, and

Hardman. They also wanted to kill John Elmer, as he was a key witness for the prosecution.

We now had an informant who was also an inmate, but jailhouse snitches are always a problem as they are hoping to get something in exchange for their assistance. The defense attorneys love to go after them for obvious reasons, particularly in serious cases like murder. The prosecutors are keenly aware of these problems, and dealing with this snitch was no exception. Through the informant, we learned that the suspects wanted proof of John Elmer's death. Since the plot to murder this key defense witness was already known, we staged a crime scene that showed John seemingly lying dead in a pool of blood, and a polaroid photo of the supposed hit was provided to the suspects.

We and the prosecutor were next on Gurule and Shelton's hit list, and they tried to hire a former inmate from the county jail to kill all three of us. At the time, they were offering $3,000 for the hit. It seemed a bit sad that our lives were only worth $3,000. With the trap set and all of the players in motion, we decided that this situation had gone far enough. The two suspects were charged with the additional crimes of conspiracy and solicitation to commit murder. These new charges were added to their long list of crimes during the original trial. John Elmer took the witness stand and said that he had helped Beach escape from prison just before Christmas of 1987. It took the jury of seven women and five men two hours and fifteen minutes to reach a verdict. The defendants were successfully convicted on all of the charges and sent to the Oregon State Penitentiary.

DENNY BRANAGAN RETIRED

On June 24, 1994, Denny Branagan retired. On his last day, he was cleaning out his locker, which symbolically held countless memories of a long successful career. I was working in uniform at that time and was in the locker room for some reason. Denny walked up to me with tears in his eyes and said, "You are the best cop I ever worked with." At that moment, we both had to walk away without exchanging another word. While I'd like to reserve judgment on that comment, it was coming from a true hero and one of my best friends. Those words meant more to me than any other medal or accolade I have received in my life.

Denny and I did a lot of dangerous assignments together. One night we were standing behind a dark house, getting ready for trouble. We were the county night detectives. Denny looked at me and said, "Does this shit scare you?" The county dope unit was getting ready to come through the front door with a search warrant, and we were asked to cover the back door in case someone ran out. I said, "Hell yes!" Putting their lives on the line and working through personal fear to serve the community is what cops do for the public every day. As mentioned earlier, Denny had been in the marine corps when his father died from a heart attack at a very young age. I think Denny had a premonition about heart issues in his family. He also passed away too young, but after retirement, he was able to spend several years enjoying life with his wonderful wife and daughters.

MEXICAN CRIME AND NARCOTICS

Portland, OR in the mid-'80s, was an interesting time, to say the least, in terms of Mexican crime and narcotics. When I was hired in 1971, Mexican dope dealers were not a factor in Portland. By the time I retired in 1997, the Mexicans and some Central Americans essentially controlled the entire narcotics trade in the U.S. There were some exceptions to this rule, but not many.

During this time, we started getting called to crime scenes where all of the parties involved were native Spanish speakers. Sgt. Bud Johnson and I caught a homicide where the victim was from Cabo San Lucas, Mexico, and all three suspects in the case were Spanish speakers. At this time, we were totally at the mercy of translators. The translator, in this case, was a Portland Police Officer who had been a missionary in a Spanish-speaking country. The officer spoke reasonable Spanish, but while listening in, I knew that we needed a detective who could speak Spanish. While a translator could deliver the basic information, I knew there were many vital pieces of information that simply got lost in translation.

This particular case was a turning point for me; I started earnestly studying Spanish during quiet moments at work and on my own personal time. I befriended a number of migrant farm workers and their families. Before long, I was regularly invited to birthday parties for young Mexican kids. Several of these Mexican parents became friends and would come to our office periodically. Throughout my career, from the time I worked with Denny forward, I would always try to work on my Spanish language skills any chance that I got. In the late 80's and early '90s, I worked with two different narcotics units. Spanish played a big part in my daily work life during this time, and the county actually sent me to an immersion language school in Cuernavaca, Mexico.

We had a wonderful relationship with immigration authorities during this time. They were good at getting the Mexican criminals held and sent home after serving their time. Eddie Fisher worked for immigration but was assigned to the Multnomah County Dope Team for many years. Eddie was one of our brothers who would assist us any time, night or day. For years, while conducting narcotics surveillance, when we saw a Mexican drug trafficker, we'd say on the radio, "We got an 'Eddie Type' out here." Rest in Peace, Eddie.

Today many local politicians will not let law enforcement work with I.C.E. This decision is a huge mistake, and we are all paying the price for such an absurd policy. Over the last decade, the price of dope has gone down, relatively speaking, and there is no shortage of drugs in our current society. Today's cops are no different than we were many years ago. They are interested in criminals no matter who they are or where they're from. Police officers don't want to harass folks because of their citizenship status. I have many Hispanic friends in my life, both in Mexico and the U.S. Although some of them are undocumented, they are all special to me, but none of them are crooks or dope dealers.

JOKE ON RAY

One of the guys that I worked with was Sgt. Bud Johnson. Bud was sort of a poster boy for the sheriff's office. He was good-looking, pumped iron regularly, had been a star athlete in college, and possessed a great sense of humor. I worked several death investigations with Bud. He had great instincts, so we never wasted time getting things done. Bud, myself, and many of our police buddies had become friends with "Uncle" Ray Lukich, owner of The Flower Drum

Tavern on 145th and SE Division, both of which I grew to know and love.

One night Ray saw Bud sitting in a booth with a female that was not his wife. They were hugging and having a grand time. Ray ran a lively night spot, so he wasn't in the business of telling patrons what they should or should not be doing. When Ray was a public figure in the bar, he was always dressed very nicely. He would often work the front door on busy weekend nights, checking I.D. and the like. If you found Ray in the club during the day, he was not so well dressed. At those times, he'd be in a t-shirt and old jeans working on the plumbing or something similar. But on this night, he was at the front door, looking sharp, greeting customers, and being Ray. Just then, Bud's wife, Shelly, came through the door. She greeted him as a friend, giving him a hug. That was the way we all felt about Ray.

Ray quickly went apoplectic, as he knew Bud was in an adjoining room with a strange woman. He started doing anything he could to distract Shelly in a vain attempt to save his friend Bud. While Ray was trying to get to the adjoining room to warn his clueless friend, Shelly was swiftly moving in Bud's direction, excited to have a drink with him. Ray was in nearly full meltdown mode as Shelly came face to face with Bud and his new lady friend. None of us could wait any longer. We had to let Ray know that the whole scenario was

170

just a gag to screw with him. Ray should have known better than to trust a group of friendly undercover cops not to set him up for a fall. The relationship between Ray and police officers in Multnomah County was what law enforcement should look like. It was an example of community policing at its best.

THE GENIUS PIMP

Another funny recollection from this time involved a beautiful young woman in her early twenties. She entered the sheriff's office to report a man who was trying to get her involved in prostitution. She apparently felt comfortable enough to share her story with us: a middle-aged man wanted to take her to Las Vegas if she would turn tricks for him. He was being persistent about this business venture, and she wanted us to get him out of her life. Without hesitation, we agreed to help her.

The man involved told her that he wanted to have sex with her, just to make sure that she was up to the task. This guy wasn't your typical pimp type, he had a retail sales job. As I recall, we had the woman record some calls with this genius of an entrepreneur, and ultimately arrangements were made for him to come to her tiny apartment one evening were Bud, Rod, and I were hiding in the bedroom.

This man, who we will call "Genius," showed up right on cue. After some small talk, the young woman convinced him that they couldn't use her bedroom for some inexplicable reason. Their business would need to take place in the living room. Genius fell for this request hook, line, and sinker. He was ready to see if this lady was up to the task of working for him in Vegas. After a few minutes, the woman gave a pre-arranged signal, and several large cops came out of her bedroom and confronted the would-be pimp. To say that Genius was surprised would be an understatement. He ultimately entered a plea to the facilitation of prostitution charge. I have often wondered how this impacted Genius for the rest of his life. I know that it helped her escape the grasp of such a low-life individual. Unfortunately, this positive outcome is not always the case in situations like these. Fortunately, this young woman had faith in law enforcement and allowed us to assist her with this unpleasant situation.

POLITICIZING LAW ENFORCEMENT

As I have worked on this book for the last two years, the role of law enforcement has become a pertinent topic of conversation. Everyone seems to have an opinion about the way police officers do their job. Each arrest or incident, no matter how big or small, is scrutinized to the most minute detail. I am here to say that I got to know thousands of men and women in police uniforms, and there is not a finer group of humans in the world. They go out every day, not sure if they will get to come home. They endure bruises, cuts, lawsuits, gunshots, tears, and exposure to the worst things that mankind has to offer. Then they wake up and go out again the next day. Law enforcement officers run towards trouble when everyone else runs away. Of course, there is the occasional bad cop, but overall in my experience, they are trying to make this world a better place.

Because of my relationship with the California Robbery Investigator's Association (C.R.I.A.) and The Oregon-Washington Lawmen's Association (O.W.L.A.), I became acquainted with a large number of law enforcement officers, from chiefs and sheriffs to beat cops and rookies. Society as we know it is doomed to a terrible future in this country if we do not provide strong support for this dedicated group of individuals.

In this current time, police are being vilified for performing their sworn duties. They have useful tools stripped from them on a regular basis by government agencies. One of the crazy rules is that police should not stop cars for minor traffic issues. This has been a valuable technique for generations, and it helps cops to keep burglaries, robberies, car prowls, and shooting incidents down. These are only a few of the benefits that derive from apprehending criminals before they are able to commit crimes.

During my twenty-six years at the sheriff's office, I saw what law enforcement should look like. The taxpayers liked us. Juries treated the system appropriately. Politicians did not spend a lot of time demonizing cops. This was all helpful in terms of making the community a safer place to live and work.

SHRINKING SHERIFF'S OFFICE

At one point, midway through my police career, the City of Portland started annexing areas of the unincorporated county. These annexed zones were on septic systems and included large parts of the county that did not have the resources to create sewer systems necessary to keep up with an increase in population density. As annexations took place, the sheriff's office was reduced in size. Ultimately, the most populated portions of the county were transferred to the City of Portland's control, and the sheriff's office became a mere shadow of its former self. The only exception to this rule was the jail deputies, who maintained their numbers.

A group of citizens formed an organization known as S.O.S. for "Save Our Sheriff's." The sheriff's office was very popular in the unincorporated areas of the county. These citizens worked hard to keep our jobs intact.

Multnomah County Deputies were liked and respected by the community because we got the job done. We weren't hampered by the silliness that legislators are pushing throughout the country today.

At the end of the day, cops are simply humans; we're like everybody else. There are times when we come home, and our wives have a honey-do list: the washing machine is broken, our bills are due, the kids need a ride, and so on. After experiencing things that most people never imagine, these seemingly trivial tasks might not seem so significant in our minds; maybe we don't give the correct response. For these oversights and shortcomings, I apologize for all of us. In my case, I was married to an emergency room nurse most of my police life, and she saw as much trauma and ugliness on any given day as I did. We could both complain about the washing machine, the bills, and a thousand other problems, but we understood each other. As I relate these stories about what cops, and nurses for that matter, do for a living, I think folks will understand how mundane tasks were not always a top priority on our list.

One of the traits that makes a good cop is the ability to become part of the community where you work. That means getting out of your prowl car and going into the bars, restaurants, and any other places where folks congregate. I did that all the time when I was working in uniform. It paid dividends many times over. Another thing I did was befriend many of the folks that I arrested, particularly those that I arrested repeatedly.

CHRISTMAS NIGHT MURDER

On Christmas Day 1985, Sgt. Bud Johnson and I were called out on a homicide case. A man named Rodney Peterson had been killed by Raymond Mitchell. Mitchell and Susan Peterson, Rodney's wife, had gone to his home in Portland to pick up her two young sons. There was a fight over custody of the kids, and shots were fired. The two suspects fled the scene. Peterson's roommate had also been shot, but he survived. These two suspects were on the run for five years.

There was a national television show called *America's Most Wanted*. The show featured Raymond Mitchell and Susan Peterson in an episode. This case was important to me, so I went back to Maryland, where the show was produced, to examine the leads that came in from the public. A neighbor who had seen the show called in and said that the suspects had been living near him in Missoula, Montana. They fled shortly after the show aired, but they were promptly arrested in Wyoming. This scenario is a good example of why I always did my best to be friends with the folks in the media.

Chapter 12

R.O.C.N. 1990-1994

In 1990, I was transferred to The Regional Organized Crime and Narcotics Task Force (R.O.C.N.) This Portland-based, federally funded task force was incredibly successful for many years. One of the reasons for this success was the fact that we had clearance for overtime work, "buy" money for dope, and cash to pay informants for intel. Although I had worked on a significant number of narcotics cases prior to this transfer, I still had a lot to learn. There were both federal and other local agency officers assigned to this unit.

Two of my long-time friends and partners were also assigned to this unit, Bob Peterson and Denny Branagan. Even though we had all been in law enforcement for years, it took us at least six months to get a firm grip on working high-level narcotics cases. For many years the drug trade was sort of segmented. At the street level, blacks had been a big part of the heroin trade. Outlaw bikers were major players in the meth business. Everyone was involved in the marijuana distribution, and there were a lot of marijuana grows in the local area. The cocaine business was almost a white-collar crime, with the one exception to this rule being crack which devastated many black neighborhoods.

INDOOR MARIJUANA GROWS

One of the interesting changes that started manifesting itself in the late 80s and early 90s was the proliferation of large indoor marijuana grows. Many of the folks running them were business types that had the money to fund all the equipment needed: grow lights, irrigation systems, property to use for the grow operation, and all the agriculture needs of the plants. During this time period, marijuana with a stronger THC content was developed. This was not the same weed that the beatniks were smoking in the 50s and 60s.

During my four years at R.O.C.N., Bert Royster from the Oregon State Police was our marijuana grow guy. Bert was probably one of the best Northwest grow experts in the law enforcement community. One of the tactics Bert used was to watch electric consumption. In many cases, if the consumption was extra high in an unlikely location, it often indicated grow lights in use. The other major tool that was used often was a thermal imaging camera which showed heat in a building where you may not expect it. I did not particularly like working the grow operations, and I definitely hated the odor associated with them. Other types of drug cases were far more dynamic. However, these growing operations often involved large seizures of cash and property, which helped fund law enforcement efforts. In these modern times, marijuana has essentially been legalized in the United States, and I do not feel that this is a positive change in our society. Thanks to the pervasiveness of the drug, accidental ingestions by young folks and even our pet population are on the rise.

MEXICAN DOPE DEALER

While at R.O.C.N., I sort of became the go-to guy when it came to Mexican dope cases. This was in large part due to the fact that I spoke limited Spanish. When I first went to R.O.C.N. in 1990, the unit was just finishing a major drug case on a dealer named Carlos Humberto Orantes Arriaga. Carlos was a significant dealer, and his case was investigated primarily by Bob Peterson and Neal Vanhorn. Neal worked for U.S. Customs at the time. Carlos was from Guatemala, and he had a major distribution network in several parts of the United States. Since I spoke the language, I was asked to interview Carlos. He was a very smooth, good-looking guy. Carlos knew that R.O.C.N. had a good case on him, so he wanted to make deals with us. He claimed that he could give us Mexican officials at the highest level as well as crooked U.S. officials on the border. The case agents did not want to make deals with Carlos, as he was the aforementioned "big fish." Consequently, he received a long sentence in federal prison.

Bob and Neal traveled all around the U.S. on this case and down to Mexico as well. Our beloved U.S. Attorney Charles Turner was not happy when the rumors started floating around that Bob and Neal had crossed the border. It was believed that Carlos and his associates distributed about eleven pounds of heroin in Seattle and Portland each month. In one case, over $220,000 was seized from couriers along with one-and-a-half pounds of heroin. Several suspects were arrested in this case, as well as Carlos. Bob and Neal were truly two of the greatest dope cops in the country.

During the mid-to-late 80s, the Mexicans started taking control of a large portion of the drug trade in the United States. At this time, they controlled most of the heroin, cocaine, and meth distribution in Portland, as well as the country at large. They attempted to take over the marijuana trade as well, but due to the agriculturists who had made U.S. and Canadian weed much more powerful than the Mexican variety, they never really captured the U.S. marijuana market.

TONY THE COLUMBIAN

While I was working at R.O.C.N. in 1992, I was contacted by an informant who told me about this guy from Colombia. Evidently, this man and his assistants were selling small quantities of cocaine in the "Fern Bars" in Portland.

These were the type of bars that catered to a more upscale clientele. Initially, we weren't particularly excited, as the mission of R.O.C.N. was to go after the "big fish." My partner at this particular time was Lenny Olson, a dope cop from the Oregon State Police.

We started conducting surveillance on several people, including a person known to us as Tony Carmona. Tony was kind of a cute, little older guy with a ponytail. He did not come across as macho or loud-mouthed as many dope dealers did. We were well prepared to deal with Tony. Our significant dope unit had all the undercover vehicles and other means of conducting surveillance that we needed. After several months, we identified at least six apartments in the Westside of Portland that were frequented by this group. Some of the apartments were being used as processing centers, while others were simply housing for this group of dope dealers. Early on, we realized that their methods were quite sophisticated.

Despite their organized operation, this group made one move that wasn't very smart. On a weekly basis, five or six of them would get in a car and go to various post offices in the Portland metro area to send money orders out. They would all walk in together and go to the various windows to buy their money orders. One of the major problems for narcotics traffickers has always been moving their money around. The I.R.S. tracks significant money movements within the banking system in the United States. This caused problems for the organized crime types in the 90s. The advent of Bitcoin and other non-traceable cryptocurrencies may be changing this fact today.

On one particular day, we followed them into the post office and watched their activity. We then got the postal inspectors involved and had narcotics dogs sniff the money for cocaine, getting lots of positive reactions. This really wasn't that big of a deal, as a large amount of U.S. currency shows evidence of narcotics, but it was helpful nonetheless. We were also able to see where the money orders were being sent with the help of these postal inspectors.

Shortly after identifying the post office operation, we started writing search warrants for all the locations involved. We searched six apartments and hotel rooms in early February of 1992. We arrested Miguel Arroyare (A.K.A. Tony Carmona,) Juana Lopez, Jorge Ivan Villa, and Manuel Antonio Valencia. All of them were from Medellin, Colombia, which was an area known for cartels and narco-trafficking.

During the searches, we found eleven pounds of cocaine and $39,000 in cash. This group was bringing in kilos of cocaine and selling it in user quantities, which was a brilliant way to maximize profits. At that time, a kilo of cocaine was selling for $18,000 or somewhere in that general price range. If the kilo was sold in partial gram quantities, it could bring in as much as $114,000. The cocaine that was being distributed by this group was about ninety percent pure, which showed how close to the source Tony Carmona was. It was coming into Miami from Medellin, Colombia, and then being transported from Miami to Portland. This group sold five or six kilos a month at a much cheaper rate than the competition. If you multiply five or six kilos by $114,000, you can see that this operation was likely operating in the range of $600,000 to $700,000 a month in 1992.

We became aware of Tony's operation almost a year before he was finally arrested. We believed, based on our informant's intel, that the group had been operating in Portland from five to eight years before we arrested them. Tony told the informant that he owned a home in Miami and a condo in Atlanta and that he flew to Portland regularly to oversee his cocaine business.

The names behind the operation mentioned above were the primary players in Portland during this time. There were others involved in repackaging the drug into smaller quantities. The sales operation revolved around pagers. When a person wanted to get their cocaine, they would page one of the dealers, who then met with them to exchange drugs for money. The drug trade at the kilo-plus level was dangerous for all of the players involved. If you had a kilo worth $18,000, there was always the possibility that someone would try to rob you. The reverse was true if you were the buyer and had $18,000 cash with you. Tony's plan was genius in terms of selling partial grams of cocaine because it avoided such problems.

We notified the D.E.A. about Tony, and in December of 1991, this agency arrested him in Atlanta on his return flight from Portland. He was carrying $16,000 in cash when he was arrested. Tony had at least nine aliases, and he was charged with forgery related to his use of a social security card in another name. He pled guilty to the forgery charge and was awaiting a deportation hearing at the time of his arrest in Portland.

After the arrest, we searched the apartment in NW Portland, where Tony lived when he was in town. The apartment was not a unit that would be considered noteworthy. It was a cute, single-story brick building. I remember interviewing the manager at the time we searched the apartment. She was pleasant with us and shocked to hear what business Tony was in. She said he was a perfect gentleman and a pleasure to have around. Tony did a good job of keeping a low profile.

CHARLES TURNER: U.S. ATTORNEY

In 1992, I was five years from retirement. I had worked with a lot of great prosecutors in many high-profile cases. I also knew a great number of criminal defense attorneys. The Tony Carmona case put me in touch with the U.S. Attorney for Oregon, Charles Turner. Charlie was a U.S. Attorney for seventeen years. He was loved by all the law enforcement types who ever worked with him. The last case that Charlie prosecuted was the Carmona group. I am not sure why he chose to personally prosecute this case, but it was a gift for Lenny Olson and me. I had prepared for a number of high-profile trials in my career, but I didn't really know what preparation was until I prepared with Charlie for war. We spent days together getting ready for trial. We would meet in his office regularly, including Saturdays. Charlie didn't need to take this case. He had a huge stable of great attorneys and could have sat in his office and watched the trial unfold, but that wasn't what he did.

Chris Peterson at his sloppy Detective Desk

Immediately upon arresting the group, we acquired all of their pagers. This fact went unannounced to the media or general public, and the pagers were ringing off the hook with everyone wanting their coke. Normally these partial gram buyers would not have gotten the attention of the U.S. Attorney's office, but Charlie decided to follow up on all the prospective buyers as well. We subsequently arrested twelve people who met up with us to buy drugs after we intercepted their pages.

Lenny and I sat with Charlie at the prosecution table during the trial. In State Court, detectives did not get to sit in the courtroom except when they testified. It was amazing to watch Charlie's legal skills, not to mention that he is the only man I have ever known who never got a wrinkle in his suit pants. I remember as we were getting ready for a trial that Charlie had offered to let Juana Lopez plead to a misdemeanor charge. I think she was Tony's wife or common-law partner, and it appeared that she was sort of along for the ride with Tony. Her defense attorney foolishly turned down the offer. Consequently, she was tried and sentenced to fifteen years in federal prison. All the primary players were convicted and sentenced to prison as well.

Charlie had once been targeted by the Rajneeshees, who were followers of Bhagwan Shree Rajneesh. They had been involved in all kinds of illegal activities, including wiretapping, immigration fraud, and the 1984 Rajneeshee bio-terror attack in Oregon. This group planned to kill Charlie and did surveillance on his home, his office, and his car. Seven followers of Rajneesh were convicted for conspiracy to assassinate Charlie. Thank God they failed. He passed away in 2018. It was a huge loss to all of us who had gotten to know and work with Charlie Turner.

STUPID COCAINE DEALER

During my four years at R.O.C.N., we always had several major cases going on at once. One of the more humorous cases involved Christian Patrick Noce. R.O.C.N. had made a drug case on Noce, and he was sentenced to prison in April of 1990. When he was arrested, police found a large quantity of cocaine and over $11,000 in cash in his Corvette. Noce was released from prison in June of 1992.

In October of that same year, Noce was out of prison and working as a delivery person for a company in Portland. On October 21, we were surveilling Noce, as we suspected he might be making some personal deliveries of drugs along with his legitimate ones for work. We had been watching him off and on for about three months when he made a legitimate work delivery to a downtown dentist's office. There was one problem with the delivery, though, as Noce inadvertently left behind an ounce of cocaine. The dentist's office called the police, and we were notified. When Noce returned to the dentist's office to reclaim his cocaine, we couldn't believe anyone could be that stupid. After this blunder on his part, we quickly wrapped up our case. Noce told Federal Judge Malcom March in 1993 that he hadn't intended on getting back into the business after prison, but he just couldn't resist it once he was free.

TRIP TO LAS VEGAS

I was preparing to leave home for work one day when my supervisor, Pat Tuley, called and asked if I could team up with Cheryl Kanzler and her partner Susie Kruger. They were doing surveillance on a man in NE Portland and had requested my assistance. I said sure, and a short time later, I met up with Susie and Cheryl. This man and his lady friend got into a car and drove directly to the Portland Airport. Cheryl and I went inside the airport, got in line behind them at the Alaska ticket counter, and found out that they were headed for Las Vegas. Cheryl asked if I would follow them to "Sin City." Of course, I said, "Yes!" At that moment, I wasn't thinking clearly, since I had not had my first cup of coffee for the day. As I was flying South to Vegas, I was thinking how nice it would've been to have some spare underwear and a shaving kit.

At that time, Alaska Airlines had phones on the plane. I thought that this was going to be interesting. How would I be able to follow this couple to their Vegas destination by myself?

With this thought in mind, I called Mr. Robbery himself, Jack Giroud, at the Robbery Homicide Division of the L.A.P.D. I explained to him that I was at thirty-five-thousand feet headed Southbound from Portland for Vegas. I was shocked to hear Jack say that the one great contact he had in Vegas had just retired. I had probably asked Jack for assistance fifteen to twenty times over the course of my career. How could he fail me now?

I called my R.O.C.N. office and whined about this silly predicament. Cheryl and Susie jumped on it before I landed, and I was told the entire Clark County, NV, Drug Task Force would be waiting for me when I got there. Sure enough, when I landed, they were there to meet me, and we followed the couple into one of the major casinos. With the help of the drug unit and the head of security for the casino, I was in the room adjacent to this couple. I did some one-man surveillance and learned bits and pieces. As long as I knew where they were staying, I wasn't too concerned about losing them.

R.O.C.N. sent someone to assist me, which helped. That day I was leaning against the adjoining wall, and the man said to his lady, "You need to be careful what you say on the phone. "Big Brother is always listening." I almost choked! This was a time before cell phones. The next morning, I told my new partner that I was going to go downstairs. I asked him to call me at one of the pay phones at the bottom of the escalator if they left the room. Much to my surprise, the woman came walking by me a few minutes later, but there had been no phone call. I was irritated that I didn't get the call, and I followed the woman to the in-house beauty shop.

As soon as I could, I called my partner and voiced my displeasure about the lack of notification. John assertively stated that she didn't leave. He said, "I can hear them having sex right now, and the man is making all kinds of sounds." The man was apparently having sex with himself. This just goes to show that some of our work could be very humorous! I became friends with the head of security at the casino and saw him every time I visited Vegas for years afterward. As it turned out, the woman was essentially a call girl. The man with her on this trip was not the same man she was working with in her criminal enterprise. That man was later arrested, charged with racketeering, and sent to prison. R.O.C.N. seized over a million dollars of assets from this suspect.

CAREER CRIMINAL OFF THE STREETS

One of the more interesting cases I had at R.O.C.N. was a narcotics case in which my D.E.A. partner Tracy Dewey and I got Phillip Charles Kellotat off of the street for the rest of his life. My research indicates that Kellotat eventually died in federal prison. Kellotat first came to our attention in 1993. When we started looking at him, he had recently been arrested for heroin possession and was basically given a pass and probation for this transgression. A Multnomah County

Judge was playing the "good guy" with drug court. Why Kellotat was treated with a wrist slap, I will never know.

Kellotat was forty-nine when we arrested him. He was charged with conspiring to manufacture and sell methamphetamine in 1993 and convicted in 1994. His life of crime started when he was a young teenager convicted of burglary. He was then convicted as an adult for burglary and robbery in California. He was arrested and convicted of a robbery in Grants Pass, Oregon, and this conviction got him sent to state prison for most of the 80s. It was believed that Kellotat controlled much of Oregon's prison drug traffic during this time.

His most publicized case came in 1987. A convicted Portland murderer named Vince Capitan was shot to death just North of Redding, CA. Kellotat was in prison at the time that Capitan was murdered, but he was still charged with the crime. Two former inmates testified at Kellotat's trial that he had hired them to kill Capitan. Another one of Kellotat's fellow inmates, Jody Seelye confessed to killing Capitan, but he refused to testify at trial, so the jury did not convict Kellotat.

After he was acquitted, Kellotat told the police that he had hired Seelye to threaten Capitan and tell him if he did anything to his wife that, they would kill him. Kellotat took responsibility for the murder and said he paid Seelye $5,000 to carry out the hit. Due to the law of double jeopardy, he could not be tried for the murder because he had already been acquitted in a court case. Kellotat was a suspect in another murder in 1987. The victim, in that case, was Tommy Hyland, who had been a fellow inmate of his in prison. Linn County officials made two attempts to have Kellotat charged for this murder, but they were both in vain. He was never indicted for this crime.

We had two informants in this case. Kellotat had been able to obtain a significant amount of ephedrine which is a precursor chemical for one method of manufacturing methamphetamine.

Associates of Kellotat ultimately testified in Federal Court that Kellotat had produced over a kilo of meth during this period of time. I went to one of his meth labs in SE Portland, and if the drug-consuming public could see the filthy conditions in that lab, it might cut down on meth addiction.

Over the years, we had done a significant amount of surveillance on Kellotat and knew his routines well. At one point, his van was being driven by a man named Duval Cox Nelson.

Someone had reportedly called the police to say that they had seen an automatic weapon resembling an Uzi in the van. The police stopped and searched the vehicle, but no gun was found. They did, however, find some drugs and precursor chemicals in the vehicle. Nelson told the police that he was helping Kellotat move from Oregon to Washington.

Our case evidence consisted mainly of taped phone calls made by informants to and from Kellotat. One of my favorite moments in this case involved Kellotat driving one afternoon from Salem to Portland on I-5. I was in one of the following cars, and we were able to hear the conversation for well over an hour between Kellotat and the informant, who was wearing a body wire. Kellotat pretty well laid out his whole case in that hour-long conversation.

Kellotat was an interesting guy in many ways. He was a stone-cold killer and a serious offender who was pretty intelligent. His trial took place in the federal courthouse in Portland. He represented himself with the help of a legal advisor, Rob Gofreddi. Kellotat had been in the "system" all of his adult life, and he was a guy who had a pretty good understanding of the law. During the trial, he was the person asking me questions when I was on the witness stand. He wasn't perfect, acting as his own defense counsel, but he did okay for a long time con. Frank Ambrose Jr. was another con involved in this case. They were both found guilty, and Kellotat was sentenced to thirty years.

I spoke with Kellotat after he was found guilty. We spent a significant amount of time shooting the breeze. He was a sad case because he was an intelligent person who had a decent appearance. He could have done a lot of positive things with his life using these innate abilities. During his trial, he told the press that his case was a "no dope, dope case." There was some truth to this statement, as we were dealing with precursor chemicals. He also said that the prosecutor, John Hoover, was a "hayseed prosecutor." That was not a good idea.

In current times, law enforcement is taking a beating for a few occasional screw-ups, and a lot of prosecutors are not doing the public any good with their terrible attitudes. Currently, local legislators have been decriminalizing many drugs and petty crimes, which can lead to greater problems overall. Phillip Kellotat was the poster child for the three strikes law. There are still arguments all over the country about this law. If you want the Phil Kellotats of the world as neighbors, keep pushing against the cops and the type of laws that make our towns and cities safer. Kellotat should never have been on the street when I made the case against him.

These tales have been a snapshot of my four years at R.O.C.N. This unit, with the strong support of the tax-paying public, was an incredibly successful task force with results that made the Portland Metropolitan area much safer than it is today.

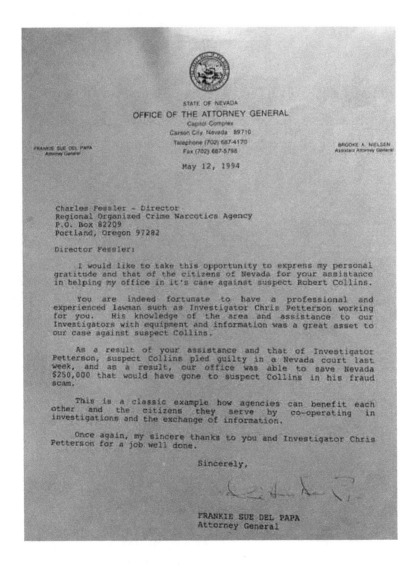

Nevada Attorney General letter of appreciation re: Robert Collins case

196

Chapter 13

After leaving R.O.C.N. in 1994, I was rotated back to patrol for a very short period of time. I was then transferred back to detectives, where I worked on person crimes for the remainder of my police career. My partner in detectives was Jim McNelly, who had a lot of time as a police officer at the sheriff's office and before that with the Newberg, OR P.D. Jim and I knew each other well, but we had not yet worked together.

Jim McNelly. MCSO - Chris's last partner in detectives at MCSO and worked the Maurin murder case investigation as a PI with Chris

The department had changed dramatically while I was away at R.O.C.N. The City of Portland had annexed huge portions of unincorporated Multnomah County due to the

197

issues of sewer systems previously noted. The patrol areas for the sheriff's office had been cut in half. It was no longer the robust two-hundred-officer department that I had joined in 1971. There was still crime and mayhem, but the number of cases that the agency saw was greatly diminished. While I was at R.O.C.N., I was working miles from the sheriff's office and generally did not know about the day-to-day activities of the department.

TAUNJA BENNETT MURDER

Taunja Bennett was a young, developmentally disabled girl who had been found murdered and dumped on a back road in Oregon's Columbia River Gorge. Although I was not aware of this case at the time, five years later, I would become all too familiar with this terrible crime. I would eventually spend significant time with her murderer, who was one of the most notorious serial killers in the United States.

Since I was assigned to R.O.C.N. early in 1990, I was not familiar with the events involving the discovery of a female body in a wooded ravine along Hwy. 30 in the Columbia River Gorge on January 22, 1990. This scenic area is about twenty-five miles from downtown Portland, and it is crowded with tourists during the summer months.

However, during the wet, cold, and windy Winter months, The Columbia River Gorge is more isolated and desolate.

On this cold winter day, a man had stopped along a ravine about one-and-a-half miles East of Crown Point and saw a female body several feet down a rugged ravine by the paved road's edge. Law enforcement was notified, and the case was assigned to Det. John Ingram of the Multnomah County Sheriff's Office and Det. Al Corson from the Oregon State Police.

The victim was wearing black boots, acid-washed jeans, a red sweater, a black t-shirt, and a dark brown jacket. Her sweater was pulled up around her chest, and her jeans were pulled down around her ankles. The fly area on her jeans had been removed. This position left her chest, stomach, hips, and legs exposed. Her jacket was open and appeared to have been partially pulled from her body, leaving her left arm almost completely outside of the sleeve. The victim had been left on her back with her body facing downhill. Her left hand was positioned alongside her body, but her right hand appeared to be elevated in an unsupported position, approximately one foot from the ground. Police discovered a Sony Walkman and a small red knife nearby. She had been badly beaten. Her face was cut and discolored; her nose and eyes were severely swollen and bloodied. There was also a rope tied tightly around her neck using a granny knot. The autopsy showed that the cause of death was manual strangulation.

There was no identification found with the victim, so finding out her identity was one of the detectives' first tasks. A sketch of the woman was released to the public, and members of her family contacted the police when they saw this drawing on January 30, 1990. They identified the victim as Taunja Bennett, a local woman who was mildly mentally challenged. Mrs. Loretta Bennett had last seen her daughter on the morning of January 21, 1990, when she left to return some rental videos. She said Taunja was carrying a Sony Walkman and a dark brown vinyl purse with a single zipper across the top and an open pocket on the side. Mrs. Bennett said Taunja also carried a small red pocket knife for protection.

Mrs. Bennett indicated that Taunja frequented several bars on the Eastside of Portland, including the B&I Tavern on SE Stark and 190th. After an extensive investigation, detectives learned that Taunja had indeed been at the B&I Tavern on the afternoon of January 21, 1990. Witnesses did not recall who she left with, but they did mention that she had her Sony Walkman on and that she must have left around 8:00 to 9:00 p.m.

WRONGFUL CONVICTION

On February 5, 1990, the sheriff's office received an anonymous call from a woman who reported that a man named John Sosnovske was overheard talking about the case at a truck stop in Wilsonville, OR. He allegedly claimed that he was responsible for the murder of the woman who had recently been found in the Columbia Gorge. A week later, a similar call came into the Clackamas County Sheriff's Office. Again, John Sosnovske was named as the main suspect in the death of Taunja. The anonymous caller said that Sosnovske was also on probation in Clackamas County.

Detectives Corson and Ingram contacted Sosnovske's probation officer, Steve Bracy, on February 14. He told them that Sosnovske's roommate, Laverne Pavlinac, had reported to him that Sosnovske had a severe drinking problem. At the request of the detectives, he made a recorded call to Pavlinac. She claimed that Sosnovske had been bragging at JB's Lounge about some dead girl and claiming that he and another man had taken her to the Vista House in the Columbia River Gorge and strangled her to death.

The next day, Corson, Ingram, and Bracy went to Pavlinac's home. Pavlinac quickly admitted to being the anonymous caller and stated that she had been living with Sosnovske since 1977. Pavlinac now said that she had heard

Sosnovske bragging to a man at JB's Lounge about strangling a mentally retarded woman and leaving her body near the Vista House. Pavlinac said that John was not home when she returned to the house on January 21 around 11:00 p.m. She said when he finally returned around 1:00 to 2:00 a.m., he took a shower which was highly unusual for him. During this interview, Pavlinac also stated that Sosnovske enjoyed playing with rope. He would threaten to rape and strangle her and verbally abuse her during sexual intercourse.

Based on these statements from Pavlinac, the police obtained a search warrant for Sosnovske's person and the condo he shared with Pavlinac. The warrant was executed on February 16, 1990. Among Sosnovske's possessions, they found a piece of paper with the handwritten phrase, "T Bennett good piece." The police also seized some of Sosnovske's hair. In a subsequent interview, Sosnovske said he had never met Taunja Bennett, and he had not killed her. Sosnovske was released later that evening. Several hours later, Pavlinac contacted Ingram and said Sosnovske told her that he may have met Bennett and forgotten. He also said he may have written her name on a piece of paper and forgotten. Pavlinac also told Ingram that Sosnovske had asked her if she was trying to frame him.

On February 20, 1990, Sosnovske agreed to take a polygraph exam. The exam was administered by O.S.P. Det. Garcia. After the exam, Garcia told Det. Corson that the results showed Sosnovske either had direct knowledge or was responsible for the murder. Sosnovske was still denying that he killed Taunja. He agreed to take a second polygraph exam. After the second exam, Garcia advised Corson that, based on the results, Sosnovske was responsible for the murder of Taunja. Corson interviewed the accused man after his second failed exam. He asked Sosnovske how he believed Taunja had been murdered, and he said, "They took the body out to the Gorge."

Sosnovske eventually said he was acquainted with Taunja and added that she was a regular at JB's Lounge. Sosnovske claimed that he saw Bennett leave the bar with his friend Chuck Riley. He went outside of the lounge a bit later and saw Riley's car in the parking lot. When he approached the car to see if Riley would give him a ride home, he saw Taunja Bennett's dead body wrapped in a blanket in the back seat. Further investigation by Ingram and Corson convinced them that Riley had nothing to do with the murder. A subsequent search of Riley's car did not reveal any evidence of Taunja's presence.

Several days later, Pavlinac contacted the detectives once again to report that she had found a purse in the trunk of her Ford Escort. She said the purse contained some cosmetics, newspaper articles about Taunja, and the fly section from a pair of acid-washed jeans. The next day it was determined that the fly section did not match Taunja Bennett's jeans. The two detectives went back to talk with Pavlinac, and she admitted that the purse belonged to her daughter and that she had cut the denim herself from the granddaughter's jeans. She continued to say that Sosnovske had murdered Taunja, but she now claimed to have helped him dispose of the body. She described dropping Sosnovske off at JB's Lounge on the evening of January 21 and said that he called her about 1:00 to 2:00 a.m. on January 22 to say that he needed help at JB's. He also told her to bring something like a blanket or plastic that wouldn't leak.

She continued her story, claiming to have arrived at JB's Lounge with a shower curtain in her back seat. She said John was between two trucks at the Burn's Brothers Truck Stop where J.B.'s Lounge was located. He was holding a piece of rope, and someone was lying near him on the ground. Pavlinac said she recognized Taunja, who had been a patient at the nearby Damasch State Hospital, where she had worked before. She alleged that John told her he had choked Bennett. According to Pavlinac, John placed Taunja in the back seat of her car on the shower curtain and told her to drive East towards the Columbia Gorge until he told her to stop. She claimed that while she drove to the Gorge, John had cut the fly section from Tanuja's jeans as a memento to remind him of the killing. John dragged the body into the woods, and when he returned to the car a few minutes later, she could see that he had an erection. As they drove back to Portland, Sosnovske allegedly threw the shower curtain out of the car and threatened to kill Pavlinac and her family if she said anything about the incident.

The next day, Pavlinac agreed to go with the detectives and show them the route that she and Sosnovske had taken on the fateful night of Taunja's death. She took them to Burn's Brother's Truck Stop in Wilsonville, OR, where she claimed to have found Sosnovske with Taunja's body. Pavlinac described Taunja's appearance in significant detail, including the fact that her face had been beaten and she had a rope around her neck.

The detectives then followed Pavlinac's instructions and drove towards the Columbia Gorge, where the body was found. As they approached the Vista House, she told the detectives to continue Eastbound. When they passed the location where Taunja was found, Pavlinac said that the area looked kind of familiar. They continued Eastbound to Latourell Park picnic ground. Pavlinac told the detectives that she recalled turning around at that location after Sosnovske disposed of Taunja's body. The group then turned around and drove back Westbound on the scenic highway. As they got to the exact spot where the body had been placed, Pavlinac said, "This here bugs me." They all got out of the car, and Pavlinac pointed to the exact spot where Taunja had been dumped. That very same day, Sosnovske was charged with murdering Taunja Bennett.

On February 26, 1990, Pavlinac again contacted Detectives Ingram and Corson. She said it was "correction time." She now wanted to change her story, saying that she had gone to her daughter's home after dropping John off at JB's Lounge on January 20, 1990. She went back to JB's to pick up Sosnovske around 10:30 p.m. When she arrived, Sosnovske was allegedly in the parking lot joking around with Taunja. Sosnovske and Bennett got into the car, but after a short period of time, the joking around ended, and a noisy disagreement ensued between the two passengers. Pavlinac then supposedly told them that she was taking Taunja home to NE Portland, but Sosnovske grabbed the steering wheel and told her to keep driving. Pavlinac told detectives that at some point during the drive, Taunja agreed to have sex with Sosnovske.

Pavlinac said that she then stopped the car at Crown Point near the Vista House, and both passengers exited the vehicle and walked away. Moments later, Sosnovske came back to the car and took her keys. He opened up the trunk and took out a piece of rope, so he could tie Taunja up while

Pavlinac watched. They walked to a doorway of the Vista House on the North side, and Taunja was allegedly lying there laughing with her pants around her ankles.

Sosnovske told Pavlinac to tie the rope tightly around Taunja's neck. She claimed to have done so while Sosnovske proceeded to have sex with her. While she was holding the rope and the two were having sex, he started hitting Taunja in the face. Pavlinac realized that after Sosnovske finished having sex with Taunja, she was dead. Pavlinac said that she then pulled up Taunja's pants and cut out the fly area so that she would be able to prove Sosnovske's involvement in the murder. Sosnovske supposedly then moved Taunja's body to the back seat, and they drove Eastbound on the scenic highway. Sosnovske then allegedly dumped Taunja in the woods, and the two drove home.

Shortly after this interview, Pavlinac was also arrested for the murder of Taunja Bennett. Despite her confession, Pavlinac entered a plea of not guilty. At her trial, Pavlinac testified that neither she nor Sosnovske had anything to do with the murder. She said that she had made up the story to get Sosnovske out of her life. The evidence against Pavlinac at trial consisted primarily of her own statements. There were a lot of details surrounding this case that was not known by the general public, but Pavlinac seemed to have known unreleased details. Pavlinac had cut a part of the fly from her granddaughter's jeans which was similar to the actual cut in Taunja's jeans. She was accurate with regard to the time of the murder, the exact spot where Taunja had been dumped, and the evidence of recent sexual activity.

After Pavlinac's trial started, Det. Ingram was notified of some writing discovered on a restroom wall in Livingston, MT, that read, "I killed Taunja Bennett. Jan 21, 1990, in Portland, Oregon. I beat her to death, raped her, and loved it. Yes, I am sick, but I enjoy myself too. People took the blame, and I am free." On February 5, a similar message was found on a restroom wall in Umatilla, OR. This one said, "I killed Taunja Bennett in Portland. Two people got the blame, so I can kill again... cut buttons off jeans as proof." The State immediately informed both the court and defense attorney about the writings. After lengthy arguments, these writings were not admitted into evidence.

On January 31, 1991, the jury returned a guilty verdict on the murder and sex charges against Pavlinac. Judge Redding imposed a life sentence with a ten-year minimum, justifying the lenient sentence because he believed that Sosnovske had influenced her behavior. Sosnovske's trial was scheduled for the following week. After Pavlinac was convicted, he changed his not guilty plea to a plea of no contest. Judge Redding sentenced Sosnovske to life with a fifteen-year minimum. The court of appeals affirmed both convictions. The writings on the restroom walls claiming to be Taunja's killer carried no significance during the trial, as any one of Pavlinac or Sosnovske's friends could have written these bathroom wall confessions in the hopes of exonerating them.

HAPPY FACE KILLER

In March of 1994, the Washington County Court received an anonymous letter indicating that the writer had killed Taunja. All the information in the letter could have come from Sosnovske or Pavlinac. On April 29, 1994, *The Oregonian* Newspaper received another anonymous letter where the writer claimed to have killed five people, including Taunja. The admissions appeared to correspond with unsolved cases. There was a smiling face scribbled on this letter, and *Oregonian* reporter Phil Stanford dubbed the author of these letters "The Happy Face Killer."

On May 6, 1994, *The Oregonian* turned the Happy Face letter over to Multnomah County Det. Jim McNelly. Jim immediately gave the letter to the State Police Crime Lab, and they developed a fingerprint and D.N.A. profile from the seal on the envelope. Unfortunately, there were no existing records that matched either piece of evidence.

A break in identifying the anonymous writer eventually came in March of 1995 when Julie Ann Winningham was murdered in Clark County, Washington. Her body was dumped on the Washington side of the Columbia River Gorge across the river from where Taunja's body was found years earlier in Oregon. Keith Hunter Jesperson was subsequently arrested for killing his girlfriend, Julie Ann Winningham. Following his arrest, Jespersen's fingerprints and blood became available for comparison purposes with the D.N.A. from the Happy Face Killer's letter.

At this point, I became involved with the Happy Face Killer Case. Jesperson was in the Clark County Jail for killing his girlfriend, and I believed he knew that his time as a free man was over. Among other things that transpired surrounding this case, he sent a letter from jail to his brother admitting to a number of other murders. This letter was turned over to the Clark County Sheriff's Office. Based on fingerprints and D.N.A. from the Happy Face Killer's letters sent to *The Oregonian*, we now had evidence that Jesperson had authored all of these letters. After his arrest in the Winningham case, Jesperson was relentless in trying to get attention about his feats as a serial killer. Even though Judge Harris from Clark County had issued a gag order with regards to the Winningham case, no one could keep Jesperson quiet.

I received a call from the Clark County Sheriff's Office explaining that Jesperson was telling stories about killing

Taunja Bennett. These stories were interesting, to say the least, but this fact took on more significance since there were already two people serving time in an Oregon prison for her killing. I went to the Clark County Jail and interviewed Jesperson. He was an interesting guy for a number of reasons. He had no prior record for anything significant. He was a huge man who did not show the usual bad guy image that I had grown accustomed to in my twenty-four years as a police officer. He came across as a big, dumb boy.

He told me that he had met Taunja at the B&I Tavern in Portland at about 2:30 p.m. on January 21, 1990. He said that when he entered the tavern, Taunja came up and hugged him. She then hugged a couple of other men in the bar. The bartender twirled her finger around her head, indicating that Taunja was crazy. Jesperson said that he then left the bar and walked to his home nearby, returning in his car later that evening. Taunja was in the parking lot of the B&I when he arrived, and she said that the restaurant next door was closed. Jesperson invited her to dinner but soon realized he didn't have enough money with him to pay for the meal. Instead, they drove to his house, where he claimed that Taunja had started kissing him. She then allegedly consented to have sex with Jesperson on the living room floor. During intercourse, Taunja said something that insulted him, so he started beating her face. He claimed that she eventually died from the physical assault, and he tied a rope around her neck around 6:00 to 6:30 p.m. He then went back to the B&I Tavern for several hours to establish an alibi. Around 10:00 p.m., Jesperson said he went home, and his girlfriend called. He spoke with her on the phone for about half an hour. He then took Taunja to the Columbia River Gorge and dumped her body.

Several of the claims Jesperson made to me about Taunja's clothing were not accurate with regard to the type and color. The general location of the dump site, Taunja's position at the crime scene, and the condition of her injuries were consistent, for the most part, with what officers found when she was located. I interviewed Jesperson at least four times. In several of those instances, I interviewed him in the Clark County Jail because he had asked to speak with me. It was blatantly obvious that Jesperson was enjoying his notoriety. At one point, he suggested that we should do a speaking tour together and teach people how not to get murdered.

There were a number of inconsistencies in the details coming from Jesperson. For example, he said that he had hit the trip meter on his car after dumping Taunja's body and that she was one-and-a-half miles from Latourell Falls. She was, in fact, .85 miles from the falls. He said he threw out Taunja's Walkman when he got back on the I-84 freeway, but this was not true. It was left near her body. Jesperson told me that, after dumping Taunja's body, he stayed awake all night at a truck stop in Troutdale, OR. When it got light, he drove to the nearby Sandy River and dumped her purse and its contents into the brush. He said the location was along the nearby scenic highway where a road veered sharply away from the river and uphill.

After my initial meeting with Jesperson, I really had no idea whether or not he had killed Taunja. At this point in my career, I had interviewed hundreds of inmates and knew to be very dubious of their claims. I met with John Bradley at the D.A.'s office in Portland. John was an experienced prosecutor and was in top management at his Multnomah County office. I told John that it was possible that we had two people in prison for a murder they didn't commit. The elected D.A. Mike Shrunk was brought in on this discussion as well.

John Bradley summoned the two career prosecutors who had tried Sosnovske and Pavlinac to his office so that I could tell them what I had heard. After listening to me, both prosecutors said we had the right people in prison. I wasn't going to argue with them at this point, as I had no idea what the truth was. This was a dilemma for sure. The issue could be ignored and may go unnoticed, but that's not what happened. This was the moment when I became a huge fan of John Bradley and Mike Shrunk. Mike Shrunk and Sheriff

Dan Noelle told me, and my partner, Jim McNelly, not to do anything besides work on this case until we had an answer. For the next month, this was all we worked on. The haunting question reverberating in our ears was, "Who killed Taunja Bennett?"

There were a lot of details to look into. Did Jesperson know the two people convicted of the Bennett murder were already in prison? Was he trying to help them out? He already knew he was going to prison for killing his girlfriend, so he didn't have much to lose by confessing to other crimes. There were several statements Jesperson made that were inconsistent with the physical findings in the case. He said that he had sex with Taunja, but this was inconsistent with the absence of any seminal fluid. He said that Taunja's teeth were protruding from her mouth after the beating, which was also inaccurate. My report was ultimately fifteen pages long. It did not say whether I thought Jesperson was innocent or guilty. It simply said that I did not have sufficient evidence to charge him in the Bennett case. We simply needed more evidence.

On October 2, 1995, a group of us, including Jesperson, Deputy D.A. McIntyre, Det. Rick Buckner from Clark County, attorney Tom Phelan, and I took an investigative trip up the Columbia River Gorge in an attempt to corroborate his story. He directed us to 18434 NE Everett

St., where he said the killing of Taunja Bennett took place. He then directed us to the nearby B&I Tavern, where he claimed to have met Taunja. We then drove to the Vista House in the Columbia River Gorge and asked Jesperson to direct us to the area where he had dumped Taunja. We got to a very distinctive hairpin turn, and Jesperson told me to keep going Eastbound. We got to Latourell Falls, and Jesperson told me to turn around and go back. We drove back to the area of the hairpin turn, parked, and all got out of the vehicle. Jesperson walked within close proximity of the dump site and said he thought this was the location where he left Taunja. He then became unsure and thought it may have been a different ravine to the South. He looked at a couple of more ravines but ultimately could not be sure which one it was. This was not unexpected, as the area is heavily forested with rugged, similar-looking ravines.

There was still the unanswered question of Taunja's purse and its contents which had never been found. Jesperson directed us back West to the Sandy River. When we reached the river, he told me to drive South on the scenic highway. We got to Neilson Rd., and he told us to stop. We were at an embankment just West of Neilson Rd. He said he threw the purse and its contents into this area which was covered with a thicket of blackberries that formed an impenetrable wall of vegetation.

On October 7, 1995, we sent a group of explorer scouts with a police supervisor to the area where Jesperson said he threw the purse and its contents. The scouts spent the entire day working in this embankment, trying to find anything that might have belonged to Taunja, but nothing helpful was located. Meanwhile, we had the State Police Crime Lab re-examine all of Taunja's clothing again, trying to find a D.N.A. link to Jesperson. Still, nothing helpful was learned.

FOUND EVIDENCE

One of the claims that Jesperson made was that, after he dumped Taunja's body, he could see it while driving away Eastbound, past the hairpin turn. On October 12, 1995, we went back to the scene and placed a mannequin where Taunja's body had been dumped. We could not see the mannequin from the other side of this hairpin turn. Detective Mike Gates then stood by the mannequin, but we couldn't see him either. This was in the Fall, so the vegetation was thicker than it would have been in December when the body had been discovered. Even taking that fact into account, it seemed unlikely that Jesperson had seen Taunja's body. The various inaccuracies in his statements and the absence of any physical evidence to corroborate his confession were problematic. It was impossible to determine with any certainty whether Jesperson was responsible for the murder of Taunja or if it had been committed by Pavlinac and Sosnovske. All of this was about to change, though.

On October 14, 1995, we sent the explorer scouts out again to the roadside embankment covered in blackberries. Although they had searched the area extensively before and had really been poking around in the dirt as they finished on the first day, my partner Jim McNelly suggested that we send them out one more time. Deputy Pat Coffeen was once again supervising the scouts. This time they found an Oregon State Identification Card, which is similar to an Oregon Driver's License that had been issued to Taunja. It was in perfect condition. The card was found in an area that had been under heavy blackberry growth for a number of years. The location of the I.D. card was essentially where Jesperson said he had thrown it. There were also several other items found nearby that were consistent with the contents of Taunja's purse.

Taunja's I.D. card was the first piece of physical evidence that we had to corroborate Jesperson's claims. The location of this crucial evidence only the killer could have known. Pavlinac never suggested that we look in this area which was several miles away from the dump site. We contacted Jesperson's former girlfriend, Roberta Ellis, who had lived with him at the NE Everett St. address in Portland from 1989 to 1991. When Detective McNelly told her that Jesperson was in jail for murder, Ellis responded, "Oh, I

217

hoped that what he told me was just a dream." She explained that one night after returning home from a trucking haul, she was trying to fall asleep. Jesperson insisted on talking to her, though, and confessed that while she was gone, he met a girl at the B&I Tavern, brought her home, and killed her. He told her it made him feel powerful.

On October 17, 1995, D.A. Jim McIntyre and I interviewed John Sosnovske in the Intensive Management Unit at the Oregon State Penitentiary. Sosnovske appeared incoherent regarding this matter and told us that he had never met Jesperson and that Taunja Bennet did not exist. It was apparent that there was no need to ask Sosnovske to take another polygraph exam. The F.B.I. then gave polygraph exams to Jesperson and Pavlinac. Hadley McCann, who administered the tests, believed that Jesperson had killed Taunja and that he did not know Pavlinac or Sosnovske. After McCann administered the exam to Pavlinac, it was his belief that she was not involved in the death of Taunja and didn't know Jesperson.

Jesperson pled guilty at trial to murdering his girlfriend in Clark County. He also pled guilty to the murder of Taunja Bennet. He is currently spending life in the Oregon State Pen. The Happy Face Killer case has intrigued the country and the world for years. There have been countless productions about this case, as well as books and numerous articles. Every year I am contacted by some news outlet or entertainment company wanting to discuss the case with me. One time a film crew came to my house with all the camera and sound equipment needed to do a production. They also brought Jesperson's adult daughter to my house without informing me beforehand. To say that I was speechless and unhappy about this incident is an understatement. To this day, Jesperson is still being interviewed by the media and entertainment industry, and he seems to relish his time in the spotlight.

KIDNAPPED BUS

At the time I was involved with the Jesperson case, I was also part of a very small detective section with the Multnomah County Sheriff's Office. The city had annexed huge portions of the unincorporated parts of the county. When I started at the M.C.S.O., we had about thirty-five detectives and a large patrol section. In 1996 we had roughly six detectives and a very small patrol section. M.C.S.O. was still a good place to work, but it was not a thriving and growing agency. The Multnomah County Sheriff's Office was disappearing as a major player in the Portland Metro area.

I was back in uniform for a brief period of time, and on August 9, 1994, I received a radio call that a C-Tran bus had been hijacked in Vancouver, WA, and was en route to Portland, OR. Another officer and I intercepted the bus on I-84, which is the freeway that goes East out of Portland. We could see the woman bus driver named Marcia Beard behind the wheel, going the speed limit Eastbound on the freeway. As the large bus rolled down the interstate, there wasn't a lot that we could do other than follow it. She took an exit at Bonneville Dam, and as luck would have it, that exit led to a dead-end road. As the bus stopped, we shot out the tires, pretty much immobilizing the vehicle. I was the first officer to reach Marcia Beard, and I grabbed her as she exited the bus. I tried to move her to safety, but she resisted my efforts. In the darkness and confusion, we did not know that the hijacker had shot himself before Beard got off the bus. We also did not know that there was an innocent sixteen-year-old male passenger still in the vehicle. Beard was resisting my efforts to move her to safety because she was fearful that we would mistake the young passenger for the hijacker. The hijacker was almost on top of the young man when he shot himself in the head. This was a traumatic event for the boy. Beard reached out to him after the fact, inviting him to ride with her on the bus, and he did. The C-Tran board adopted a resolution in May of 1995 and praised Beard for her heroic actions.

Chapter 14

THRILL KILL ON LARCH MOUNTAIN

On October 2, 1996, my views on the world of crime were jolted in a big way. I thought I had seen it all, but that was about the change. Jim McNelly and I were still at work around 6:40 p.m. that day when uniformed officers were dispatched to a remote area in the Columbia River Gorge. The location was Palmer Mill Rd., about a quarter of a mile North of Larch Mountain Rd. The call was about a shooting, and the initial information was that two kids had been shot and were down on the ground. Information came in quickly that there were two vehicles potentially associated with the scene. One of them was an orange VW Rabbit, and the other was a small, white Chevy pickup.

This area of Larch Mt. is remote, and communication via radios or cell phones is often challenging. A number of Multnomah County deputies and Gresham Police Department officers quickly arrived in the area of the scene. My partner Detective Jim McNelly arrived at 9:00 p.m., sealed the area off with crime scene tape, and called for the Oregon State Crime Lab (O.S.P.) All we really knew at the outset of this investigation was that there were two gunshot wound victims. The area where the shooting took place had frequently been used over the years as a gun range for target practice. Upon stepping out of a vehicle in this area, you were likely walking on spent shell casings that had been left there for generations.

At 10:30 p.m. Jim and the Deputy Medical Examiner proceeded to the crime scene. Up to this point, we did not know who the victims were. One of them was lying face down near a target and some mounds of dirt. The other shooting victim was lying near a pickup on his side. The victims were identified as forty-eight-year-old James Boyles and thirty-six-year-old Ronald Dunwoody. At 11:00 p.m., the O.S.P. Crime Lab arrived with four crime scene personnel and started processing the scene, working until 5:00 a.m. the next day. Shortly after the bodies were identified, Detective Copeland from Troutdale P.D. and I responded to the home of Ron Dunwoody at 178th and NE Oregon St. We met his wife at the door, explaining that her husband had been killed and she was now a widow.

OCTOBER 3, 1996, 11:30 P.M. KEVIN & GARY GREGORY

Jim McNelly received a call from the radio room that a possible witness had called from NE 26th St. in Gresham, OR, and two cars were dispatched to this location. Jim sent Det. Budge and Det. Reiser to the location as well, and I soon followed. Sgt. Chris Herron was one of the Gresham cars to arrive at the residence. He knew that there had been a shooting and had some general information regarding the victims. He also knew that an orange VW Bug had been observed at the scene of the shooting by witnesses, but it was no longer there. When he arrived at the Gresham address, there was an orange VW Bug in the driveway.

Officers made contact with Gary Gregory and his son Kevin at home, and Gary informed the police that his eighteen-year-old son had something to tell them. Kevin told officers Herron and Hucke that he and his two friends had gone up Larch Mountain to shoot guns, and they started talking with two guys who were already shooting at the makeshift range. Kevin said he heard a gun go off, and when he turned around, one of the men they had been talking with had been shot. At this point, the Gresham officers wrapped up their involvement in the investigation. Since they now believed this young man was a suspect, they awaited the arrival of detectives. Kevin showed Sgt. Herron, the two rifles they had taken with them to shoot that day. Both rifles were in cases in the garage.

Shortly thereafter, Detectives Budge and Reiser arrived and asked Kevin if he had shot anyone. Kevin said, "Yes." He was once again advised of his rights, and then he started talking about that fateful day. Kevin Gregory told Det. Budge that he and two of his friends had gone shooting on

Larch Mountain at about sunset. He identified his friends as eighteen-year-old Cory Lewis and nineteen-year-old David Cook. Kevin said that he had taken two of his father's guns with him. They were identified as a .308 rifle and an AR15. Kevin said the guns were now in the garage at his home. With the assistance of Kevin's father, Gary Gregory, the suspect's firearms were recovered and taken into possession by law enforcement. Sometime later, Gary actually asked me if he could keep the .308, as elk season was coming. When he was told that he couldn't, he then asked to at least keep the scope, and he was again told no. The Volkswagen was also taken from the residence as evidence in the homicide case.

Kevin Gregory told Det. Budge and others that David Cook was shooting the AR15, Cory Lewis was shooting Dave's gun, and he was shooting the .308. He said that about a half-an-hour after they had arrived, two other men showed up. Kevin said that all five of them had been casually talking. He learned that the man in the white shirt was an ammunition reloader, as he had been picking up brass to reload. Kevin said, "David told me the guy in the white shirt pulled his gun up and pointed it at him, so he unloaded his weapon on the man."

At this point in time, there were a lot of moving parts to this case. Guns were being taken into custody, the VW was being towed, and interviews with Kevin were in full swing. When I contacted the wife of one of the victims, Cathleen Dunwoody, at her home, she told me that her husband, Ron, had asked her if she would mind him going to shoot at the range. She said that it was okay with her, so he left with a man named James Boyles, who was staying with the couple while in the process of selling his Portland house.

I arrived at the Gregory house with Det. Copeland at about midnight. Gary Gregory confirmed all the information about the guns and where they had been kept after his son Kevin returned from Larch Mountain. I interviewed Kevin's girlfriend, Brenda Drinkard, who was living in the Gregory family home at the time. She told me that she had been present when Kevin, Dave Cook, and Cory Lewis left the house to go shooting. She was also at the house when the three returned together later that day. Drinkard was most helpful in providing phone numbers for Dave Cook and Cory Lewis. Det. Budge, and I took Kevin for a ride, and he pointed out the residences of Cory Lewis and David Cook in Portland's Parkrose neighborhood. He was then transported to the office, where I conducted a recorded interview with him.

OCTOBER 3, 1996, 1:30 A.M. KEVIN GREGORY FORMAL INTERVIEW

I was able to sit down in my office with Det. Budge and conduct a formal taped interview with Kevin Gregory. Gregory told me that he called the police earlier in the evening because his father had come into his room and awakened him saying something about a shooting on Larch Mountain. His dad knew that he had been up there the previous week and thought maybe he had also been up there that night. The described location was just a gravel pit where people went to shoot for target practice. He said that he had been there with Cory Lewis and David Cook. They had been there for a short period of time when two guys showed up in a blue-gray pickup. He said they were just shooting at the junk that was lying around, and they continued shooting as the men arrived. The three of them talked to the two arrivals and had a general conversation that was all friendly. He referred to the two guys as younger and older.

The two men set some targets up. Kevin said when the new guys started shooting at their targets, he and Cory were watching them see how the grouping of their shots looked on the targets. He said that he and Cory walked away a short distance, and then he heard a bunch of shots. He looked back, and the older guy was lying on the ground while the younger guy was holding a gun in his hand and looking at him.

He said the younger guy, later identified as Dunwoody, was by his friend as he looked towards Kevin. Kevin said he unslung his gun because he thought the young guy was going to shoot him. The young guy then jumped behind a pile of dirt, and Kevin believed that he might have been shot. He said he then saw David Cook run into the woods with his father's AR-15. He thought that David had shot both persons. Kevin said he also ran into the woods, and when he came out, he saw the younger guy lying on the ground by the pickup. Kevin said he could see blood on the man, and one of his arms was moving. I asked him what he did then. His answer was, "Well, I sat there and watched him for a minute, and then I don't remember what went through my head, but I shot him."

When asked what he thought when he shot the man, he said, "I must have felt sorry for him and was trying to put him out of his misery." He said the rifle had a scope on it, and when he shot from seventy-five to one-hundred yards away, he put the crosshairs on the man's head. He did not see the man move again after the shot. He said he then ran to his car, and when he started driving away, his friends came out of the woods and got into the vehicle. When they were driving away, David reported he had seen the younger guy point his .357 toward Cory and Kevin, so he shot him.

During my conversations with Kevin Gregory, he made a statement on tape saying that he had been treated well during the time of his arrest as well as during his interviews. I knew that we had three suspects and two victims. We had a significant crime scene, and several agencies were assisting us. There were three arrests we had to deal with. On October 3, 1996, at 4:00 a.m. Cory Lewis was arrested at his home and brought to my office. It was becoming quite a long day. After I advised Cory Lewis of his rights, I asked him if he had been treated well when he was arrested and up until our interview started. His statement was, "Actually, both officers were extremely polite."

This was my last significant case as a police officer. I would like to believe that my skills as a felony investigator were top-notch and that, whenever possible, I knew that a low-key, pleasant approach was the way to go. There were times when that did not work, but in this case, we obtained the desired results. After thirty years in law enforcement, I knew that following chaotic, stressful, and often very dangerous events, there would be a bevy of attorneys who would have weeks, months, or even years to study our methods and try to destroy our cases. One of the tools I did not want to give to the defense attorneys was the fact that I had lost my temper, abused someone, or was not honest. This is why I always got a taped statement from each suspect as to how they were treated during the arrest and at the ensuing interview.

OCTOBER 3, 1996, 4:00 A.M. CORY LEWIS FORMAL INTERVIEW

I started interviewing Cory in my office with the assistance of John Copeland from Troutdale P.D. Cory stated that he knew David Cook, but he did not know Kevin's last name. He said they did take this trip to Larch Mountain together around 3:00 p.m. the previous day. The three of them met up at his place at 11181 NE Weidler St. in Portland. He said that their first stop was a gun store where they purchased ammunition for three different guns. One of the guns belonged to David Cook; it was a MAC 91 or a version of an AK47. He said he purchased eighty rounds of ammo for the MAC 91. He said that Cook bought .308 rounds and rounds for the AR15. He also said that the AR15 was what David had used to shoot the men.

Cory said that they went to Kevin's house after purchasing the ammo. Kevin changed out of his good clothes and picked up the AR15 and the .308. The three of them then drove up Larch Mountain to shoot. When they got in the area, Dave and Kevin started telling Cory that the two of them had been shooting in the same area the previous Monday. They told Cory that there had been a group of eight

Mexicans up there with a lot of guns, including some automatic firearms. Cory said that Dave and Kevin told him they would like to have shot the Mexicans if they had the AR15 and the .308 with them at the time.

I stopped Cory during the recorded interview, as I wanted to ensure that I understood what he was saying. He confirmed that Kevin and David would have wanted to kill the Mexicans if they had adequate weapons for the job. I then asked, "Okay, and did they tell you that if they had an opportunity on this particular trip, they were going to shoot somebody." Cory answered, "Yes, they did." I asked Cory if that talk scared him a bit. He said it did, but he felt like it was difficult to just get out of the car. He said that if he did something Dave didn't like that Dave would probably just kill him. I asked why he felt that way, and he said, "David told me that was what he would do." Cory confirmed this incredible story again.

Cory said Kevin and David were in the front seat en route to Larch Mountain, and he was in the back seat. He said that the stereo was loud, so he couldn't hear all the conversation in the front seat. He said that when they arrived at the gravel pit, they all got out and fired a few shots. Cory said he had the MAC 91 with a twenty-round magazine. Dave had the AR15, and Kevin had the .308. Cory said that they found a road sign lying along the road, picked it up, and took it to the area where they planned on shooting. They then all took turns shooting into the sign.

They heard a vehicle approaching, and it turned out to be a bluish-colored pickup with two men in the cab. One was older, and one was younger. They stopped at the gravel pit area and got out. Cory said he looked at Dave and Keith, and the two smiled at each other. Several times during the interview, Cory referred to Kevin as Keith. I think that their friendship was new, and at times he used the incorrect name. Cory said the young guy, identified as Dunwoody, got out of the truck and was soon picking up spent brass off of the ground. They all visited for a few minutes. Dunwoody saw that Dave had .223 bullets for an AR15 and said he was collecting rounds. Dunwoody asked if he could have one of the rounds, and Dave gave him a live .223 bullet for his collection. The older guy, identified as Boyles, was just visiting and mentioned that he was thinking about doing some reloading of shells himself. After the five men visited for a few minutes, the newcomers decided to put up some target stands to begin shooting. Cory says he fired a few more shots at the sign with his AR15.

A short time later, Kevin, Cory, and Dave were back near their car. According to Cory, Dave and Kevin were talking about shooting the guys. Cory asked, "Well are you guys going to do it?" And they said, "Yeah." Cory said he fired a few more shots at the sign while the newcomers were both practicing with handguns. Cory said that he, Kevin, and the two newcomers went down to the area where they had been shooting and examined their targets. Dave went back towards their car and reloaded his magazine. Cory said that he and Kevin started walking back toward their car, and all of a sudden, shots rang out. Dave had shot both of the men. Cory said he believed the older guy was dead but that, the younger guy was still alive.

According to Cory, the three of them ran into the woods nearby and got together. Cory said to Dave, "What the hell did you do that for?" Dave told him, "I told you I was going to shoot him." Cory said he did not want to offend Dave, as he was really pumped up talking about how good it felt to shoot someone. He thought that Dave still had one full clip. Cory said Dave started trying to explain things when they heard Kevin's gun go off. They started walking back towards the Volkswagen, and they heard Kevin shoot three or four more shots.

Cory said he then heard a vehicle coming down the road, stopping for two or three seconds and then taking off. Cory said they all got into the VW, and he was in the backseat trying to get the guns covered up. They left the area and started to drive back towards Corbett and home. They went to Kevin's house and hid the .308 and the AR15 in his garage. They then got back into the VW and drove to Cook's home in Portland's Parkrose neighborhood.

Cook changed his clothes and called his cousin to see if he could hide his gun at the relative's house for a while. Corey discovered that Cook had eighteen thirty-round magazines that he wanted to hide as well. They got into Cook's Plymouth Duster and went to his cousin's house near 105th and NE Wygant St. with the MAC 91, Cook's boots, and his clothes. Cook and Kevin talked with the person in the house. Cory was not sure if it was his cousin or brother. This person suggested that the gun be taken to Dave's mother's house in North Portland, so the trio drove there, and all went inside. Dave told his mother and her boyfriend that someone had pointed a gun at them, and they had to shoot the man in self-defense. Cory said that he also lied to Dave's mom just to keep their stories lined up.

At this point in the recorded interview, I stopped Cory and asked, "Did you see Dave point the gun and pull the trigger?" His answer was, "Yes, I did." He said that he was walking away from the two people when he saw Dave start shooting, and the two men dropped to the ground after being shot. Cory said that neither of the men made any threatening move. When asked a second time, he confirmed that neither of these men did anything that could have been seen as threatening. I then said to Cory, "I am going to characterize this in my own words. It sounds like a thrill killing. Is that what this killing was all about?" Cory said, "Dave seemed to enjoy it very much, and he was really pumped up after the killing." This ugly case was referred to several times in the local media as the Thrill Killing.

I then asked Cory how many times he thought Kevin shot, and he said about five or six times. He said that Kevin thought he hit the younger man once. That story changed a bit, as Cory thought he shot the younger man once in the leg when he was getting into his truck. According to Cory, the man dropped his gun and said something like, "No more." The man was then lying on the ground, and Kevin said he shot him in the head. Cory said that while the three of them were at Dave Cook's mother's place in Portland, the mother's boyfriend was there as well. There was a lot of discussion on the topic of making up a story about the killings. This story centered around the lie that Cook had told his mother about the men pointing guns in a threatening manner. They left Dave's gun at his mother's house.

At about 5:00 a.m. I was still interviewing Cory Lewis. I said, "Let's talk about your involvement up there. Are we going to find any slugs from your gun in those deceased people?" He said, "When Dave shot, I turned around and shot." He said that both men were close together when he shot from the hip two or three times. I asked him whom he thought he hit, and he said the younger guy. He wasn't sure if he had hit the older guy. I asked him why he thought he hit the younger guy, and he said he saw a couple of spots on his back when he shot. I told him that he had kind of painted Dave as a bloodthirsty person, so why did he shoot? He replied that he wasn't sure what Dave and Kevin were going to do. Cory said, "When I saw Dave fire, I turned around and fired."

I asked Cory if there had been a discussion about killing someone between himself, Kevin, and Dave as they drove to Larch Mountain to go shooting last evening. His answer was, "Yes, we did." Cory said that Kevin and David had asked him, "If someone was up there would you shoot them?" Cory said that he didn't know if he could do it or not, but he hoped no one would show up before they ran out of ammunition. I again asked Cory if the three of them had discussed killing someone as they drove to Larch Mountain, and once again, he said, "Yes." My interview with Cory ended at 5:20 a.m.

OCTOBER 3, 1996, 5:45 A.M. DAVID COOK FORMAL INTERVIEW

I started my interview with David Cook on October 3, 1996, at 5:45 a.m. Det. Monte Reiser and Det. Jim McNelly participated in this interview as well. The interview took place in my office at 122nd and NE Glisan St. in Portland.

Cook had already been advised of his rights several times, but I did it one more time just to be thorough with my procedure. He agreed to speak with me. After a bit of chitchat, I asked him if he had been up on Larch Mountain the day before, and he said, "Yeah." I then asked him if he was up there when two people got shot. His answer was, "I don't remember. I spaced it. I don't even remember where I put my wallet." We talked about the wallet comment for a short time, and I tried to get him back on track. He was asked if he remembered getting into Kevin's VW that afternoon. He corrected me and said, "Yesterday, yeah." He said he went downtown with Kevin and got an application for a position as a police data entry technician.

Cook rambled on a bit more, talking about how he and Kevin were just screwing around and going to get something to eat. He said Cory joined them after he got off of work. I asked him what the three of them were doing yesterday around 5:00 p.m. He said that he didn't look at his watch. I then asked him what they were doing after it started to get dark. He said, "We went over to my mom's and talked about doing some yard work." Cook kept being evasive. There was then a short conversation about his time in the military. He said that he got kicked out because he wasn't a team player and all the other people were jerks. When I asked him if he knew what a MAC 91 was, he said, "Yeah, that's my rifle."

236

I then asked him if he had taken the gun and his clothes to his mother's house and what her name and address was.

I asked him if he thought Kevin and Cory would lie to me. Essentially, he said they had both been honest with him. I told him the basics of what Kevin and Cory had told me. He finally admitted that the three of them had gone to Larch Mountain in Kevin's VW. He said he couldn't remember what time it was. I asked him if he remembered loading up some guns at Kevin's house, and he did have a recollection of that. He said that he purchased the MAC 91 at Three Bears gun shop about four months ago. He also said that he bought twenty clips for the gun.

He was then asked about seeing a group of Mexicans shooting in the same area previously. He recalled the Mexicans shooting a gun that he thought was automatic. He implied that the Mexicans made him nervous, so he left the area.

I again asked him if they had gone to Larch Mountain yesterday, and his answer was, "I know we went up there." He described the area where the shooting took place, and he talked about the firearms that he and his friends had with them. He was continuously evasive but finally admitted he had been shooting the AR15. He was asked if they had picked up a sign and taken it up with them to use as a target, to which he replied, "Ask Kevin and Cory. I don't remember." He also couldn't remember how long they were up on Larch Mountain. After a number of nonsensical answers, he said to me, "We didn't shoot anybody, did we?" He was speaking in low tones and mumbling a lot. I asked him, "If someone got killed up there yesterday, what would be the reason?" His answer was, "It would be self-defense."

I was not present when Cook was arrested at his home. Our dope unit was tasked with making the arrest, and I learned afterwards that there had been some indications that Cook had been making a pipe bomb. That information had been passed on to me, and I asked Cook about it. He downplayed the pipe bomb questions and said that some old guy told him that if you shoot at black powder, you can make it blow up.

He kept saying he couldn't remember anything and was making a lot of mumbling. I asked why his friends had better memories than he did. He then implied that he suffered from blackouts. I asked him if he had been using narcotics or alcohol, and he said that he had smoked marijuana once. He then told me that he had run his head into lots of things over the years. There continued to be lots of mumbling and no real answers to most of my questions. After twenty-five minutes of not getting anywhere, I asked Cook if his conscience was bothering him. He said, "I don't know if I did it." I said, "What would it take to convince you?" His answer was, "I don't know, maybe if Kevin and Cory told me." I was glad that he suggested this idea, as I thought it might get him to tell the truth if he was confronted with it.

A couple of minutes later, I had my partner Jim McNelly bring Cory Lewis into the room. Det. Budge came into the room as well. Cory was pleasant and trying to be helpful. It should be noted that Cory was never promised anything for his help. I asked Cory for a brief synopsis of the events of the day before. In the presence of Cook, Cory told the story again. He talked about Kevin and Dave coming to his house to pick him up. He described going to Three Bears and buying ammunition. He talked about going to Kevin's house and picking up guns. He spoke about the drive up to Larch Mountain. He talked about going to the rock quarry with Dave and Kevin. At one point, I interrupted him and asked if he had previously told me on tape that he and his friends had a conversation about killing someone as they drove to Larch Mountain. He said, "Yes." Cory again told the story in detail while Cook and the detectives listened. I asked Dave if this was refreshing his memory. He said, "I don't remember. I don't think that I would shoot anybody." I asked Cook if Cory was just lying to us, and he continued saying that he didn't remember.

Cory continued, saying that Dave had gotten out of the car and picked up the traffic sign that they used for target practice. Cory spoke in detail about who had which gun. He talked about Dave putting the sign up on a berm to shoot at it. He mentioned that Dave had the AR15. Dave, at one point earlier, had said that we would likely find his fingerprints on the sign. I asked him at this point if he still thought we would find his fingerprints on the sign. His answer was, "Look, I don't know." In the presence of Dave and the detectives, Cory again described the two victims arriving at the gravel pit and their activities when they arrived. I again asked Cook if any of this had helped to refresh his memory, and he said, "No." Cory Lewis did a good job of trying to add all the details that were significant, including taking the MAC 91 to Cook's mother's place. None of this was helping with Cook's memory.

There was no doubt what Cook's game was. At 6:21 a.m. I told Cook that Jim McNelly was going to talk with him because he had tuckered me out. Jim asked Cook some general questions like where he lived, where he went to school, and what kind of student he was. Jim then asked him what he did yesterday, and his answer was, "Well, I guess I shot someone." Jim then asked Cook if he had ever lost his memory before. Cook replied, "Yeah. I forget stuff all the time." At 6:32 a.m., the tape was turned off, and shortly thereafter, I left the room.

At 7:15 a.m., Jim and Monte Reiser started interviewing Cook again and recording it. Initially, there was a lot I don't remember. After some mumbling and more confusion, Cook said, "I was walking back, and the guy was pointing the gun at Kevin and Cory. I just...I am out of ammo... took the bolt back. I am like, 'Whoa,' and I stopped, and I ran into the bushes, and I sat there, and I didn't know what to do, I am like, 'Uhhh.' And I think there was some more gunshots, I don't remember hearing anything." Jim asked him, "What happened to the guy after your gun was empty? Did you see him then?" His answer was, "I think they fell."

Cook stayed with the story that one of the men had pointed his gun in the direction of Cory and Kevin. He then said he had just emptied his gun on them. Cook finally described in some detail all their activities after the shooting. He talked about taking his gun to his mother's house and returning the VW as well as the guns to Kevin's house. He said he only shot once and emptied the thirty-round magazine. After leaving this frustrating first interview with David Cook, I knew that I needed some more time with Kevin Gregory.

At about 6:45 a.m., on October 3rd, I was talking to Kevin Gregory again. Detective John Copeland and Deputy Greg Lange were also present. Gregory had been in a holding cell in our office. When I saw him, it looked like he had just woken up. I told Kevin that I had been speaking with his friends and that there were several issues that I wanted to clarify. I asked Kevin several times if there had been a discussion about killing someone yesterday, and he kept saying no. He said that Dave talked about wanting to kill someone so much that he sort of tuned it out.

Kevin again said that he and Cory had been looking at the targets, and as they started walking away, shots rang out. He said when he looked, the older guy was on the ground, and the younger guy was not standing upright but still had a gun in his hand. Kevin said that he ran into the forest for a while. I asked him, "What happened next?" He said, "I was in the forest for a while; I don't know exactly how long. When I started to come out, I noticed the guy laying by a truck, and I saw from his shoulder to his elbow, and it was moving, and uh, his shirt was all bloody, and I took aim and shot him." I asked Kevin if the guy was pointing a gun at him, and he said, "I don't think so, but I know it was in his hand." Kevin talked about his gun having a scope and indicated that he shot the man in the head.

Kevin again confirmed going to Dave's mother's place and working on a plan A and a plan B alibi with the mother and her boyfriend. I asked Kevin if either plan involved calling the police, and he said, "No." When pushed about the original shooting by Dave, Kevin said that he thought Dave had shot them just to shoot somebody. Kevin said that when his father heard about the shootings on the news, he came into his room and woke him up. His father couldn't find one of his guns and discussed the missing firearm and some missing ammunition with Kevin. Kevin told his father about the shooting but stuck to the story of someone pointing a gun at them. The father had heard on the news about an orange VW being seen in the area of the shooting, and the description matched his son's car.

Dozens of interviews were conducted during this case. There was a significant amount of forensic work done by the State Police Crime Lab. Jim McNelly and I flew to Phoenix and interviewed one of Cory Lewis's aunts. One of the things we learned from this interview was that the trio all played the game Dungeons and Dragons. We had heard that information from other sources as well. This case seemed airtight and well put together. We had confessions from everyone, although Cook's confession could have been better.

THE TRIAL

October 2, 1996, was a terrible day for two victims and their families. We spent the next several months getting ready for the trial. I retired in June of 1997, and the trial started in December of that year. Homicide cases do not end the day you make an arrest; that is actually the day when the work becomes intensive. There was so much work to do prior to the trial, so the D.A.'s office just hired me as an investigator. When I wasn't involved in trial preparation, I would go out and serve subpoenas on all kinds of unrelated cases for the D.A.'s office. The D.A.'s office was like a second home to me for many years, and the attorneys and staff were certainly a big part of my life.

On December 10, 1997, I was on the witness stand in Judge Ellis's courtroom for most of the day. The prosecutors were John Bradley, who was the number two attorney in the office, and Bill Williams. Bill went on to be the U.S. Attorney for the District of Oregon for a number of years. The defense attorneys for the three defendants were Mr. Dickison, Mr. Jones, and Des Connall. Des had been the elected District Attorney in the early 70s in Multnomah County. I had a number of court cases with Des over the years, so I knew him reasonably well. I did not like him, but he always earned his money when representing clients. I did not know the other attorneys.

This was the last time that I was going to be on the witness stand as a cop. I had a lot of practice on the witness stand over the previous thirty years at the sheriff's office and through my limited experience in the air force. I had been involved in a large number of high-profile cases in both state and federal court. From my point of view, I was a fine witness for the prosecution. The entire case was revisited while I was on the stand with the prosecution. Des Connall was pretty routine with me, and he knew me well enough to know that he couldn't cause me to derail the case. Dickison was another matter. We had never met previously. He would constantly make questionable comments, hoping that I would agree with them. That didn't happen.

There was a Reid Training Program that taught police officers ways to conduct interviews. There was a lot of effort by the defense to attack statements made to police if those officers had taken the Reid course. I had not taken that course, nor had I ever taken a course on interrogation or interviewing. Dickison tried to go down that rabbit hole with me. He was the most irritating attorney that I had ever been in court with. Dickison was constantly combative, and I do not think he accomplished much. There were pages and pages of confession transcriptions that were reviewed a number of times. Mr. Jones was reasonably pleasant with me while I was on the witness stand. He covered a lot of ground, but none of it was problematic for me. This case involved multiple police officers from several agencies working for one common goal: to send three killers to the state pen for murder, and that is what eventually happened.

A CAREER FULFILLED

When I got off of the witness stand on December 10, 1997, I was done with my law enforcement career. I had arrested hundreds of bad guys and sent many of them to prison. I had received excellent legal training in regard to giving Miranda warnings, and that was helpful in this case. When there are defendants in the courtroom on serious charges, there are always correction officers present for obvious reasons. On December 10, 1997, one of the corrections officers who had sat through this lengthy trial came up to me in the hallway and told me that he thought I had done a great job on the witness stand during the many hours that I was in the "hot seat." Little did this officer know how much I appreciated that compliment.

When I actually retired in June of 1997, one of my long-time friends and mentors, Sgt. Jack Giroud came to Portland for my retirement and spent some time at my home. At this point in time, Jack was still employed in the Robbery Homicide Division at L.A.P.D. In June of 1997, Jack was in year forty-one in his L.A.P.D. career, and he went on to do another ten years. Jack had driven my personal car to the office that morning as I drove my detective car to work for the final time. As Jack and I drove away from my office at 122nd and NE Glisan St., tears ran down my cheeks. I was leaving an agency that I dearly loved. I was driving away from friends that I had known for twenty-six years. I was exiting a career that had exceeded all of my expectations as a Multnomah County Deputy. One of the few people in the world who could understand my tears was seated in the car with me.

Chris retiring - 1997

PART III

Chapter 15

PRIVATE INVESTIGATOR: 1997 - PRESENT

The life of a private investigator had always interested me, and after retirement, I got my chance to try it. Having never really been in the business world and not knowing much about it, I had a lot to learn. Suddenly, I did not have a crime lab to help me with those pesky forensic problems. I did not have an airplane and six seasoned investigators to conduct mobile surveillance. I was not surrounded by dozens of agencies that were always happy to assist when I got in over my head. I did not have a word processing pool to assist with all the reports involved in conducting a proper investigation. I barely even knew how to turn the computer on. What was I thinking?

During my law enforcement career, there were not many occasions to observe what private investigators did. There were a few exceptions to this rule, however, and one of those involved former Southern California Detective Al Vetter. Al was a close friend of Jack Giroud, which is how the introduction between us was initially made. Al moved to Portland in the early 70s and was head of security for a large corporation in the city. When that closed down, Al drifted a bit and then heard about a job opening with Georgios in L.A.

Within a few years, Al was traveling the world chasing counterfeiters in the fragrance industry, discovering which organized crime gangs were involved, and making connections with N.Y.P.D. I learned a lot about the industry listening to Al and became friends with N.Y.P.D. Detective Jimmy Golden who Al worked with on these counterfeit operations. Another of my mentors was Jack Heslop, who was retired from Scotland Yard. Jack traveled the world as a P.I. for many years, and I learned a lot about the scope of international P.I. work from him. Both Al and Jack were close personal friends, and we were all guests in each other's homes over the years. Early in my career, I did some work for Al in Mexico.

One day I was listening to Al and Jack when one said to the other, "When you go to Singapore next, be sure and say hi to Suzie." She was a musician who was performing in one of their favorite piano bars in Singapore. Jack worked on all kinds of interesting cases, from counterfeit leather goods produced in Italy to high-tech counterfeit products manufactured in China. On another case, Jack had to determine why ships leaving New Orleans were sinking with scrap metal bound for South America. Their assignments were highly varied, to say the least.

I initially had illusions of becoming the next James Bond in the P.I. world. I assumed that I could get over my "not so 007" appearance issues! I soon learned that the fast-paced world of international crime investigation was not coming my way. There were a couple of reasons for this fact. One was that, with a few exceptions, Portland was not a center for world commerce. Another issue was that federal law enforcement retirees had international connections that I simply did not have.

My first "toe in the water" of private investigation involved getting licensed in Oregon and Washington and getting insurance. Those weren't particularly challenging; check that off of the list. Next, I needed clients, and I wasn't sure where to find them. I had sense enough to put a P.I. ad in the local newspaper, *The Columbian*. I initially wondered where I should put the ad and decided on the business section. The ad ran for a month while I sat at home close to the phone, pen poised in hand, awaiting the onslaught of calls that were yet to come. When the phone finally rang in response to my thirty-day ad that cost me $500, it was a very sweet lady who was looking for a job. So much for my first steps in the exciting life of a P.I.

I also placed an ad in the Multnomah County Bar Association publication. That got the attention of a Portland law firm. They became my first regular clients and sent work to me most months for the rest of my P.I. career. The change in what I did for a living was very pronounced. I was the Lone Ranger all of a sudden. My previous work in the air force and the sheriff's office was dynamic and fast-moving for the most part. It was very lonely in my new P.I. world, but the work started slowly trickling in. Several of my friends from local and federal law enforcement got into the business, which made my new way of life seem more normal.

TRIP TO YELAPA AND PUERTO VALLARTA, MEXICO

A couple of years before my retirement, the county sent me to a Spanish Language School in Cuernavaca, Mexico. Also, while I was still employed with the sheriff's office, I sent myself to a language school in Puerto Vallarta, Mexico. I instantly fell in love with P.V. and started making annual trips to my new "second home." One winter after I retired, I was in P.V., and a fellow P.I. Dennis Chaney was contacted by a Portland law firm to get an important message to a witness who was living in Yelapa, Mexico. Dennis knew that I was in Mexico and that Yelapa was close to P.V., so he contacted me.

Yelapa is a beautiful beach town fifteen to twenty miles South of P.V., and it is an interesting place for several reasons. Folklore has it that a number of draft dodgers during the Vietnam era ended up in Yelapa and married local ladies. It is a small village with a distinct American area and a separate Mexican area. The only issue with this case was that Yelapa, although not an island, can only be reached by boat. I hired a panga, which is a large twenty-foot fiberglass boat, to take me to Yelapa for eight-hundred-and-fifty pesos. This was my first full day in P.V., so I was as white as a sheet and looked a lot like a tourist. There was no dock, so I looked like General MacArthur storming the Philippines when I got out of the panga and waded ashore.

I walked up to Juanita's Bar on the beach, which consisted of four large posts buried in the sand with a canvas cover to help keep the ice chest a bit cooler. There were only male patrons in Juanita's. All of them were Anglo, mostly unshaven, with skin that had seen a lot of suns. I suspected that some of the patrons were left over from the Vietnam conflict, and if I had to guess, some of the others might have had outstanding arrest warrants in the U.S. As one can imagine, my whiteness stuck out like a sore thumb. I told them that I was looking for a woman named Suzie, as I needed to give her a message.

One of the patrons looked away from his beer and pointed to a blackboard that was fifty yards away from that fine dining restaurant and cocktail lounge. He told me that I could leave my message on that board. If anyone was interested in speaking with me, they would get in touch. I pondered that for a minute and decided there may be a better use of my vacation time than sitting and waiting for the reply. I walked a couple of hundred yards into the Mexican neighborhood and went into a small bodega that was Yelapa's version of a 7-11.

I told the proprietor in Spanish that I was looking for Suzie, as I needed to give her a message. There was a young Mexican boy in the bodega, and he knew Suzie's kids. The proprietor told me that Luis would take me to Suzie's house for fifty pesos, which I happily paid. Five minutes later, I delivered the message to Suzie's house and was en route back to P.V. on the panga express. Suzie's house was only about two-hundred yards from Juanita's. This episode confirmed my thoughts about the clientele at Juanita's cocktail lounge.

PROCESS SERVICE FROM A CAB: PUERTO VALLARTA, MEXICO

Several years later, another Portland attorney requested my services in P.V. The attorney represented Marie Nauman from Bend, Oregon, whose father had pled guilty to two counts of first-degree sex abuse in 1992. Ms. Nauman and her sister were his victims. Her father had received five years probation for the offense, and she did not feel that justice was done. Ms. Nauman filed a civil suit in 2001 seeking $7,000,000 from her father and a suit for $2,000,000 against her mother, alleging that she knew of the abuse and failed to protect her daughters. This suit was languishing because the parents had moved to Puerto Vallarta, Mexico, and could not be located to serve court papers. In March of 2002, a person who knew the defendants saw them in P.V. and notified Ms. Nauman's attorney. At about the same time, another couple from Bend saw the parents in P.V. as well. Again, it came to the attention of the Portland law firm representing Ms. Nauman that the parents were in Mexico, so I was tasked on March 21, 2002, with locating and serving the defendants in P.V.

At this time, I had been going to P.V. for five years and had made a good friend named Abe. Abe grew up in P.V. and was well-connected in town. I told him about my mission, but he did not want to get personally involved. Mexico can get dangerous, particularly if you are going up against people with money. Abe did introduce me to one of his good friends who had been a local cab driver for a long time. After a brief conversation with the cab driver, I felt that I had just met the P.V. 007. Our first step was to go to the condo where the defendants had been living prior to being recognized by the people from Bend. My Spanish was not perfect, so I sent 007 into the complex to speak with the

Mexican staff working there. Within a brief period of time, 007 was back, and he told me that we needed to go to Colonia Gaviotas, which was only a couple of miles away.

We started surveillance on a house that we believed the couple had recently moved into. In a short time, we saw the defendants leaving the gated grounds in a vehicle with Oregon plates. Keep in mind that my surveillance was taking place in a yellow cab. I got out of the cab and walked up to Nauman's vehicle, convinced that we had identified the correct people. I handed the summons and complaint to the woman on the passenger side of the vehicle. They denied being the parents of Marie Nauman. Mrs. Nauman immediately threw the documents back out of the window and sped off. I picked them up, placed them under the gate to the house, and we left. My wife and partner got a good photo of me presenting the documents, another one of the papers flying out of the window, and then a final one of the court summons being placed on the property.

P.V. 007 continued his work, and soon we knew where the defendants were likely banking and what their business was in the Marina district. It was unclear what results would come from the earlier process service. Marie Nauman said, "Winning a judgment even without money would be a victory." She said of her parents, "What I'd be most satisfied with would be if they came and faced me in court."

INTERNATIONAL SERVICE

Another time, I was contacted by a Seattle attorney who was trying to locate a man in Puerto Vallarta in order to serve him papers. He told me that the man he was seeking had left some information in his abandoned Seattle office. Some of this information appeared to be an address in Puerto Vallarta. Evidently, this man had bilked a large number of folks in some type of time-share scam. The attorney told me that he wanted to locate the man in order to go through the international requirements for getting him legally served in Mexico.

In the P.I. business, getting paid often means taking a leap of faith. In crime movies and novels, the P.I. gets an assignment, solves the matter quickly, and goes away a hero. The exchange of money never comes up. Being the client of a P.I. is also taking a leap of faith. This is particularly true if you will likely only use the P.I. one time. The Seattle attorney was clearly concerned about paying for an international trip when he did not know what to expect from me. I made him an offer. I told him that there would be one fixed price if I failed and a different fixed price if I was successful. He agreed to these terms, and off I went to consult my friend Abe in P.V. again.

In P.V., street addresses can be difficult to locate if you do not know the Colonia or neighborhood, where the address is located. Addresses are much different than those in the U.S. The address found on a scrap of paper in the man's abandoned desk proved to be difficult to find. Abe and I finally found the address, and of course, it was in a gated community. As luck would have it, there was a home for sale in this gated community. We contacted a realtor who was happy to take us for a tour. As we were touring the house, I looked down the street and saw a vehicle parked in front of the suspect's house. The vehicle had an Arizona license plate. I told the realtor that I wanted to talk to a neighbor about the gated community, and away I went.

The owner of the house came to the door with his five Boston Terriers and his young Mexican wife. We visited for several minutes, and I left. I called a P.I. in Arizona and asked her to run the AZ license plate for me. The plate had expired for several years, but it came back to the person of interest. I contacted the Seattle attorney and told him what I had learned, including the name of the man's wife as well as the names of several of those cute Boston Terriers. After this thorough investigation, the attorney paid me the "successful fixed rate."

MORDIDA

Over the course of my career as a P.I., I have done several cases in Mexico, but I am always careful about what I do down there. Life can be cheap in Mexico; that being said, I feel much safer on the streets of P.V. than I do on the streets of Portland, OR, today. Corruption, or "mordida," is rampant in Mexico. It is not uncommon for journalists, politicians, cops, and sometimes everyday folks to get murdered in Mexico with no repercussions. The money involved with the drug trade is hard for most of us to comprehend. Cops in Mexico are not paid well; thus, the temptation for bribery is common. On the other hand, cops in the U.S. are generally paid appropriately well, and the corruption issue is not as common. The main question is: do we want well-paid cops who are professionals, or do we take what we can get when all of the good ones are driven away?

One time I was asked to go to a Mexican attorney's office in Puerto Vallarta. My friend Abe felt that my language skills might be necessary for this meeting. However, the attorney spoke good English, and it was immediately clear that the proceedings would be corrupt. The person who greased the palms of the judge with the most money would likely win this civil matter in the local courthouse. Professional, honest judges are of the utmost importance, and we should look at police officers the same way. The vision that I had about world travel and exciting investigations never materialized, but I did enjoy several trips to Mexico that were subsidized by clients. My dreams of Monte Carlo, London night clubs, and cruising on the Mediterranean may have never happened, but the next twenty-three years were still interesting, challenging, and educational.

Once my P.I. business was up to speed, I averaged fifty to one-hundred cases each year. Many of those cases were as simple as finding an address for someone so that they could be served some sort of legal document. I have probably had two-thousand cases as a P.I. Most of them were mundane, but some of them were infinitely more interesting.

EAST MEETS WEST SIXTY-ONE YEARS LATER

My father went to Ricks College in Rexburg, Idaho, in his early years. While he was there, he met a female Japanese student. They became casual friends, and when the war broke out, his female friend returned to Japan. She spoke English as a second language. My father later continued his education in Utah, where he received his bachelor's degree. On December 7, 1941, my dad was just finishing his formal education when Pearl Harbor was bombed. At the time of the bombing, dad was in the hills of Southern Idaho, near Firth getting a Christmas tree. Shortly thereafter, he enlisted in the navy and was soon being trained in a new field known as radar. After completing his radar training, he was sent to U.S. Navy O.C.S. and was commissioned as an ensign in the navy in February of 1944. He spent WWII in the South Pacific until Japan surrendered on September 2, 1945.

Shortly after the surrender in 1945, dad was in Tokyo working for the U.S. Navy High Command as a glorified courier. One day he was given a message to take to a Japanese official. He was informed that his interpreter would meet him outside at the door of the hotel, and she would assist him with any needed interpretation. He went outside to meet his interpreter, and there was his Japanese friend from Ricks college. The year 1945, WWII history, and East meets West would again become part of our lives in early 2002.

In March 2002, Dai Ichi Travel of Portland opened a Tokyo branch. Shortly after the branch was opened, a Japanese woman contacted the travel agency in Tokyo and said she wanted to go to Portland to find a man she had known in Japan during the war. The woman had a faded photo of the man that was taken sixty years earlier, and she had not seen or heard from the man since the photo was taken. She knew that his name was Robert Mitchell. She also knew that his father had been a dentist and Robert liked to tap dance.

The woman was Sumiko Irie, and she spoke no English. Sumiko prepared a letter in Japanese and sent it to the Portland office of Dai Ichi Travel. Ultimately the letter was given to Nami Soesbe to translate. The letter read in part that she had met Robert Mitchell in the Yamamoto Hotel in Fukuoka, Japan, where she was working in 1945. She said her house was five miles from the hotel. She thought Robert was two or three years older than she was.

Robert had nicknamed her "Dimples," and they became friends and possibly felt a spark impossible to explore because of circumstances, language, and cultural differences. Sumiko and Robert were only alone once for about half an hour. They tried to communicate using a Japanese/ English dictionary. Robert was walking her home and gave her a kiss which she said surprised her. Her father was very strict, and this whole thing was relatively awkward. After the kiss, Robert Mitchell completed his tour and went home to the U.S. Sumiko was sad and surprised when she learned that he had gone home. Mitchell sent four letters to Sumiko, and he eagerly waited for her response which never came.

In Sumiko's letter to the travel agency, she said, "I am so disappointed in myself." She explained that her parents and her husband were dead and that her children and sister were encouraging her to go to Portland and look for Mr.

Mitchell. She said that her husband had just giggled and smiled when she told him about her past experience with Mitchell. In the letter to Dai Ichi Travel, she said she was a little embarrassed and did not want to cause any trouble. She just wanted to express her appreciation for Robert's kindness. Nami Soesbe at the travel agency reached out to me to see what I could do. There was a limited budget, and I burned through the funds quickly. My wife Diana and I spent hours in various libraries trying to find a dentist named Mitchell, from Oregon, during the war in 1945. I discovered that was a common name, as we found about one-hundred Robert Mitchells who was about the right age.

I had a good friend named Tom Hallman, who was a Pulitzer Prize-winning journalist at *The Oregonian* newspaper. I told him about this interesting tale, hoping that Tom would take the bait and run with the story. Tom spoke with someone at the legal department for the paper and said that he couldn't do what I needed. I'm sure there were conversations about an adult child in Japan or something similar. I had really exhausted all reasonable avenues, but with Tom's insight, I decided to run a display ad on Sunday, July 13, 2003. The ad was about two-by-three inches wide and read as follows: "Looking for Robert Mitchell. Were you in Fukuoka, Japan, in the army in 1945? Was your dad a dentist in Oregon? Did you like to tap dance?" There was a blurry photo of Robert Mitchell, which had been provided to

263

me by Nami. Shortly after the Sunday paper came out, my phone started ringing. Surprisingly, at least two of the calls were from the grown children of Robert Mitchell. I'm sure they were wondering about siblings in Japan as well.

The following Sunday, this story was on the front page of *The Oregonian*. Robert Mitchell had been married for fifty-two years, his wife's name was Jean, and they had eight children. Robert was living in NE Portland. My wife and I were quickly invited to the Mitchell home and were treated like longtime friends. We learned that Robert's kids were all familiar with "Dimples." They had learned about her while rooting about in a box of Robert's army memorabilia stored in the attic. Robert Mitchell told me that after my display ad came out in the paper, his kids showed up and started grilling him. They said they were only joking, but they still wanted to know if there was a fifty-eight-year-old sibling someplace across the ocean. Bob's wife, Jean, was delighted that their friendship had been renewed. She knew they were just kids caught up in a war. Jean went on to say, "She was probably so sweet and genuine, just like he was. They saw that in each other, and that's very lovely."

Shortly after the newspaper article came out, Sumiko Irie came to Portland and had a wonderful reunion with Robert Mitchell and most of his family. I have never seen a more joyous gathering, and it did my heart good to know that I had been instrumental in making this reunion happen. This case was very meaningful to me. Robert Mitchell and Sumiko Irie were friends in Japan in 1945. My dad was in Japan at the same time, coming across a young Japanese girl that he had been friends with in college several time zones away. The following Christmas, Peterson Investigations received several beautiful, small gifts from Sumiko. This incident just goes to show that there are a lot of nice people in our world. The Sumiko Irie matter was likely solved because of my relationship with the local newspaper and my friend Tom Hallman at *The Oregonian*.

The translator of the initial letter that got this case started, Nami Soesbe, was twenty-eight years old at the time this story was developing. Nami said that this whole situation might seem strange to Americans. She had grown up in Japan, however, and Sumiko reminded her of her grandmother. Nami Soesbe eventually moved back to Japan after our case. She was living and working in Tokyo. We met and had dinner with her and her son in 2006 when we were in Japan during our Semester at Sea voyage.

M.V. EXPLORER/ SEMESTER AT SEA/ TRIP AROUND THE WORLD

In 2006 I was hired as a security person to work on a ship for three months. The ship was the M.V. Explorer, and it was retrofitted as a floating university that circumnavigated the world twice a year in the Spring and Fall. A total of six-hundred university students from around the world were taking classes on this ship for a semester. The program was known as "Semester at Sea." The voyage I was on left Ensenada, Mexico, in August of 2006 and arrived in Fort Lauderdale, FL, one-hundred-and-five days later in December. We stopped for three to five days each in Japan, Hong Kong, Vietnam, Burma, India, Egypt, Turkey, Croatia, and Spain.

My job on the M.V. Explorer was essentially that of a security guard trying to keep college kids safe. At that time, these students made you proud. I investigated a number of minor issues and a few significant ones. For the most part, it was an uneventful job and a very interesting look at the world. I would normally get up at 11:00 a.m., have lunch at noon, and then go to a staff meeting at 1:00 p.m. My staff meeting involved those who were responsible for student life on the ship. The director of that group had a Ph.D., and all of his eleven-person staff had at least a master's degree. I was the only lightweight person in the group with my bachelor's degree in Police Science. I would attend the classes being offered on board when it was convenient, but I always missed the morning classes because I was sleeping. I would often not go to bed until 2:30 or 3:00 a.m. I wanted to put my kids to bed safely, particularly if it had been a Pub Night.

As we were approaching Japan, one of the professors onboard was giving a lecture about the country. Because I was sleeping, I missed his early morning lecture. He was an expert, as he spoke fluent Japanese and had lived in Japan for a number of years. This particular afternoon, I walked into a highly educated group of people for my required staff meeting. Most of this staff was female, and my immediate assessment was that they were all angry and stressed to the max.

After listening and watching the pandemonium for a few minutes, I was finally able to ask the question, "What happened?" It took a couple of minutes for one of the cooler heads to tell me. Evidently, in that morning's lecture, the professor had referred to the Japanese as Orientals. Showing my ignorance, I asked, "And so?!" That is when I learned how vile that word was to this group of educators. Being a dumb ex-cop and farm boy, I had somehow missed that update in my education. I pondered this weighty issue for several days and decided that when I got back to America, I needed to inform all of the owners of restaurants with the name Oriental in them that they had better change their signage.

MAURIN MURDERS: COLD CASE

In late 2003 or early 2004, I was contacted by Gordon Spanski, who was the under-sheriff of the Lewis County Sheriff's Office in Washington. My former partner Jim McNelly and I knew Gordon before retirement, and we had all stayed in touch. Lewis County is one of the biggest counties in the U.S., encompassing two-thousand four-hundred and thirty-six square miles. The bulk of the county is covered in Douglas Fir trees with some agriculture. Logging has been a mainstay in the county for a number of years. The population in 1985 was sparse, likely around seventy-five-thousand people in this large land mass. A high percentage of the working people were involved in logging in Washington and fishing in Alaska. The county seat is Chehalis which is a picturesque, small town with a classic-looking courthouse that has been around for many generations.

For me, the Maurin murder case started in the Lewis County Sheriff's Office and ended in the Lewis County Courthouse. Gordon Spanski contacted Jim McNelly and me, asking if we were interested in looking into a 1985 homicide that had perplexed the sheriff's office in Lewis County for almost twenty-five years. We told him that we were, in fact, interested and were soon introduced to one of the more honorable people that I had ever met. That man was

Dennis Hadaller, whose mother and stepfather, Ed and Minnie Maurin, were brutally murdered on December 19, 1985.

Ironically, at the time we met Dennis, he was a county commissioner in Lewis County. As I looked at his business card, I was a bit shocked to see that his home phone number was on the card. He felt that he was a public servant and took his job seriously. Our first meeting with Dennis took place in the sheriff's office. The sheriff and his top management were all present, and many of them had been working detectives at the time that Ed and Minnie Maurin were murdered.

At the outset of this investigation, we learned about the horrible event that took the lives of these two beloved community members. On December 19th, 1985, Minnie Maurin's daughter Hazel Oberg notified the sheriff's office that her mother and stepfather, Ed Maurin, were missing from their rural home on U.S. Hwy. 12 in Ethel, WA. When guests started arriving at the Maurin house on the 19th for a planned social event with family and church friends, the couple wasn't home, and their vehicle was missing.

An immediate search of the area was conducted, and nothing of significance was found. A neighbor across the street thought he had seen the Maurin vehicle leave on the morning of the 19th, and he believed it had gone Westbound towards Chehalis and I-5. On December 20, 1985, at about 8:00 a.m., an employee of Yard Bird's Shopping Center found the Maurin vehicle in the parking lot with the keys in the ignition. The employee also noted large blood stains all over the inside of the vehicle. Detectives from the sheriff's office soon took over the investigation, and it was immediately in full gear.

Witnesses believed that they had seen the Maurin vehicle traveling West on US Hwy. 12 and then North towards Chehalis. They believed the vehicle was being operated by an elderly man with an elderly female in the front passenger seat. The Maurins were in their eighties. It was also believed that a younger white male was in the back of the car, resting his arm on the bench seat in front. It appeared that the young man was talking to the people in the front seat.

As news got around town, the Sterling Savings and Loan became a focal point. Mrs. Hull, who was a bank employee, knew the Maurins as they were customers of the bank. This employee had some significant information that she related to the police. On December 19th, she received a call from Ed Maurin at about 9:35 a.m. He said he needed $8,500 in cash as "the kids" were going to help them buy a car. Ed came into the bank about an hour later, but the teller did not have the cash put together yet and told Ed that it would be just a few minutes. He returned to his car, which was parked several feet from the bank door. The bank employee went outside after the money was ready and motioned for Ed to come in and get his cash. The bank employee thought there was another person in Ed's car but did not notice who it was. Ed was given his money in $100 bills.

Another witness reported seeing the Maurin vehicle sometime after 10:30 a.m. as it proceeded West from Chehalis on State Hwy. 6. This was going away from town and the Maurin residence. Witnesses were consistent, with an older man driving and a younger man in the back seat. The younger man was consistently described as wearing a dark stocking hat with dark hair.

On December 19th at about 11:30 a.m., Deputy Forth of Lewis County observed the Maurin vehicle when it came to a stop at Bunker Creek Rd. and State Hwy. 6. Deputy Forth later recalled that the vehicle was stopped for an unusual amount of time, as there was no oncoming traffic. Deputy Forth approached the vehicle from the rear and got a partial view of the driver in the rear-view mirror. The driver was a white male wearing a dark stocking cap with dark hair. At this time, the fact that a crime had been committed involving this car was unknown.

Years later, Deputy Forth was shown a "mug throw down," and he picked the photo of Ricky Riffe as being the most likely person he had seen in the Maurin vehicle on December 19, 1985. That vehicle was a 1969 Chrysler Newport, and it was found around noon the same day at the Yard Birds parking lot in Centralia. The sheriff's office responded to the Maurin vehicle, and while processing it, a large amount of blood was discovered, which was determined to be that of the Maurins. A hat was determined to be Ed's, and shotgun pellets were also found in the vehicle.

Subsequent to locating the vehicle, Sherri Amell and a friend reported that on December 19, 1985, at about 11:45 a.m., they were at Yard Bird's getting ready to pull out of the NE corner of the parking lot, which was the exit to Kresky Ave. They both reported that they saw a young white male with dark hair wearing a stocking cap and green army coat walk directly in front of their vehicle. They believed the male might have been carrying some type of long gun wrapped in something white. They both assisted in preparing a sketch of this person.

On Christmas Eve 1985, at about 9:00 a.m., Mike Haunreiter reported finding a body just off the end of Stearns Hill Rd. This road runs off of Bunker Creek Rd. and is about seven miles West of Chehalis in a very rural part of Lewis

County. The responding deputies found the two bodies of Ed and Minnie Maurin. Crime scene analysis revealed that the Maurins were both shots while in the front seat of the car before being dragged outside the car and left. A lab analysis of the shotgun slugs revealed that they were 00 buckshot, likely from a 12-gauge shotgun. A drawing composite was shown to the public based on observations by the witnesses at Yard Birds. Several individuals appeared to be possible suspects, but after a significant number of investigations, no viable suspect surfaced.

The town was devastated by the murder of these two highly loved and respected members of the community. When Dennis Hadaller said goodbye to his mother at the funeral, he put his hand on her casket and said he would not forget her; he didn't. In February 1991, an informant came forward and contacted Deputy Jack Hill, telling him that Rick Riffe was involved in the Maurin murders. Hill lived in the Mossy Rock area and knew Rick Rife and his wife, Robin. Hill had not seen the Riffe's in several years. In March, Detectives located Robin Riffe, who was in an Arizona prison for a 1989 burglary conviction.

On March 28, 1991, Lewis County Det. Neiser spoke with Robin on the phone. He told her that he was investigating an old homicide case. Robin responded, "You mean the one where two old people were killed?" Robin made it clear that she was afraid of Rick Riffe and had concerns for herself and her family. After some discussion, Robin agreed to provide more information. She told the detectives that she was married to Rick in December of 1985. She said they were living in a mobile home near Filbert Rd. on Hwy. 12. This was about seven miles East of the Maurin home.

She told Det. Neiser that sometime in December of 1985, she took Rick and his brother John Riffe to a small grocery store on Hwy. 12 in Ethel. The store was about three miles from the Maurin residence. They were supposed to burglarize the store, and then she was going to come back and pick them up. She drove a short distance away, smoked some weed, and did some cocaine. She said that when she went back to get them, they were not there. She said Rick and John were both wearing stocking caps, and John was wearing a green army jacket. Robin went home when she could not find Rick and John. She admitted that her memory was clouded because she was using a lot of drugs at the time.

Robin said that when Rick and John returned to the residence where she and Rick were living, they had blood on them. She recalled that they went to an area near Mayfield Lake and disposed of their bloody clothes. Robin recalled counting $8,600 in cash with both men. Det. Neiser had not provided the aforementioned dollar amount to Robin. She continued explaining that during the evening after the money was counted, the three of them drove to White Pass and purchased $4,400 worth of cocaine from Ralph Vickers. In April of 1991, two Lewis County Detectives contacted Vickers, who was in the federal prison in Sheridan, Oregon. Vickers recalled the drug deal involving Robin at White Pass. He recalled being paid with $100 bills. Vickers said that he was unhappy with Robin because she brought a stranger to the deal. He subsequently identified the stranger as John Riffe.

Early in April of 1991, Det. Loop contacted Les George, who was a friend of Robin and Rick. Robin told Detectives that Les had loaned a shotgun to Rick in 1985. Les George quickly told Det. Loop that he thought Rick had murdered the Maurins. Les George went on to relate that he was a long-haul trucker. He recalled getting a message to call Robin through his employer's dispatch on December 19, 1985. He called Robin after midnight on December 20th from a payphone in Fergus Falls, Minnesota. He said Robin was upset and said, "You won't believe what Rick has done." George heard a noise in the background, and Rick got on the phone to ask why Les was calling. When Les explained that he was simply returning Robin's call, Rick quickly indicated nothing was wrong and hung up the phone.

George told detectives that he had purchased a shotgun at Yard Birds sometime before December 1985. He said he had given it to Rick Riffe to cut it down, so he could carry it as a "cab gun" in his truck. He had trouble getting the gun back, and it wasn't returned until two or three months after the Maurin murders. Les George provided some significant information aside from the shotgun. He said that in December of 1985, he was going through a divorce and was doing drugs with Rick Riffe and his brother John. He said that the Riffes were broke in the early part of December, but when he got back from his trucking run to Minnesota, he learned that Rick Riffe had purchased an expensive boat typically used for commercial fishing.

George also recalled that a couple of weeks before the Maurin murders, he, Rick, and John Riffe were in a vehicle and passed the Maurin residence. The Maurins were outside, and George said that they must have a lot of money. He said that their son Dennis Hadaller had a successful logging business nearby, and the Maurins owned the Christmas tree farm around their home. George also told Det. Loop, "I bet they were shot with 00 bucks." He went on to say that is the only type of ammunition that he had seen Rick Riffe use with the shotgun. He said when he finally got the shotgun back from Rick Riffe, he left the gun with his stepfather Richard Sandecki. Detectives contacted Sandecki, and he confirmed that the gun had come into his possession. He said he didn't want the gun around the house, so he threw it off the Mayfield Lake Bridge. Numerous efforts were subsequently made to find the gun, including military divers, but it was never found.

Detectives confirmed with Yard Bird's employees that Les George had purchased a shotgun from them on October 3, 1984. Detectives also interviewed Robin's father, Robert Vessey. Her father recalled Rick cutting off the barrel of a single-shot 12-gauge shotgun in 1985. Detectives once again flew to Phoenix and interviewed Robin Riffe in prison. She admitted to withholding information during the first interview. She said she was scared of being charged with a crime and feared Rick Riffe. Robin said her previous story about dropping the Riffes off at a store was true. She also confirmed that she had used some drugs. A short time later, she went back to the store, but the Riffes were not around, so she returned to her home.

She said that the next morning after the kids had gone to school, John Riffe called and told her to pick him up at Mary's Corner off of Hwy. 12. This was six miles from where she had dropped them off the previous evening. She picked John up, and they drove to the Bunker Creek area. Robin said John had blood on his clothes, and when asked about it, he said they'd shot a deer. She said the Riffes had previously lived in the Bunker Creek area, which was later confirmed by detectives. Robin said that John stopped at a turn-around on Bunker Creek Road. They got out of the car and walked a short distance down the gravel road. Robin then saw the body of a woman lying on the ground. At the same time that she saw the woman, she saw Rick walk out of the woods carrying a shotgun similar to the one owned by Les George.

Robin said she "freaked" when she saw the woman and started running back to the car. Rick told John to get Robin out of there or to get rid of her. Robin told detectives that she had seen another person at the scene, whom she described as a large, white male that she had never seen before. Despite a significant effort on the part of Lewis County detectives and myself, we never identified or confirmed this third male's presence. Robin Riffe confirmed that the sketch composite from the Yard Bird sightings looked more like Rick than John. Unfortunately, Robin died from natural causes a short time after her statements, so no further interviews could be conducted.

In February 2004, I interviewed a Lindsey "Butch" Senter. Butch said that on the day of the abduction, he was driving by the Maurin residence and saw two men wearing dark clothes and stocking caps. Senter said it looked like one of the men had a gun wrapped in something white. By the middle of March 2004, the most significant piece of information in the case turned up. When Jim and I were hired by Dennis Hadaller, we all attended a meeting at the sheriff's office. I brought my friend Tom Hallman, the Pulitzer Prize-winning journalist from *The Oregonian*. Tom was interested in the story. As it turned out, Tom decided not to immediately run with the story for several reasons.

Jim and I were working closely with the Lewis County Detectives, and we had really become a part of that team. We were issued identification that was needed to come and go from their office, and, more importantly, we knew where the coffee machine was. Jim and I did not have any relationship with the local paper, but we plunged headfirst into our story with them anyway. In short, the paper reported that the Maurin murders were being investigated by two private investigators rather than the community's police force. The local detectives were not happy with the Lewis county paper, but nonetheless, this article had the desired effect.

A short time later, Jason Shriver called Dennis Hadaller and told him what he had seen at the time of the murders. Jason grew up in Lewis County and was quite familiar with the Mossy Rock area where the Riffes had been living at various times. Jason had read about our efforts in the local paper, so Dennis listened to him and then immediately called to tell me about his statements. Afterward, Jim and I quickly had an in-person interview with Jason Shriver on March 18,

2004. Jason had two reasons for initially withholding this information from the authorities. He was afraid that the Riffe brothers would kill him, and he also told us that his mother was afraid and had asked him not to say anything. She may have called the anonymous tip line before and gotten no response; no one can be certain about this fact. Jason told us that his mother had recently passed away, and he finally felt at liberty to tell his terrible story.

Jason told us that in December of 1985, he and his mother were driving into Chehalis when they passed the Maurin vehicle headed Westbound on Hwy. 12. Jason said that he had encouraged his mother to pass their car, as the vehicle in front of them was going slow, and he was on the way to a dentist appointment. He said that he saw John Riffe in the vehicle with an elderly couple as they passed the car. Jason did not know the Maurins, but he recalled waving and getting a good look at John Riffe in their car.

A short time after the murders, John Riffe contacted Shriver outside of the Mossy Rock theater, which Jason's family owned. Jason said the man threatened his life if he said anything about what he had seen. Shriver told us that his friend Gary Newberry witnessed the threat from John. On May 15, 2004, I interviewed Gary, and he recalled the incident at the theater with his friend Jason but said he did not actually hear the threats. It is noteworthy that the Riffe brothers were well known in the region, and people were fearful of them.

I interviewed a woman who had lived with Rick Riffe for three to four years during the time of the homicide. She was terrified to speak with me about Rick, as she felt it could be very dangerous for her if he found out. She spoke about how Rick had smashed her son's fingers with a hammer and then burned them with a lighter. She said Rick beat her regularly when they were together, but she was afraid to make an issue out of it. They had moved to Alaska in 1987 or 1988. One time when they were in Alaska after her daughter had wet her pants, Rick held her head in the toilet and flushed it.

We knew that John and Rick Riffe had moved to Alaska sometime after the murders. I ran newspaper ads in Southeastern Alaskan newspapers offering a $10,000 reward for information on the Washington State murders. I targeted areas where I knew the Riffe brothers were connected or had been living. Jim McNelly and I interviewed dozens of witnesses for an entire year. One of the witnesses that we worked hard on was Les George, who was thought to have been the owner of the murder weapon. He likely knew more than he was telling us. I flew to Minnesota and interviewed another person of interest. About the time that Jason Shriver contacted us with the major piece of information regarding his observations, Bruce Kimsey with the sheriff's office came on board the investigation. Bruce and I flew to Alaska together and interviewed a number of Riffe's associates.

As we poked around in Alaska, one of the interesting items discovered was the fact that a woman named Lisa Bailey was living in the state with John Riffe. Shortly before Christmas in 1995, Lisa called her mother in Lewis County and said words to the effect of, "I know they did it, and I am coming home." Lisa's mother believed this comment was in relation to the Maurin murders. Lisa had previously purchased an airline ticket for a young relative to come and visit her for Christmas, and she was excited about the upcoming plan. Shortly after this phone call between mother and daughter, Lisa died from a gunshot to the head. I interviewed a nearby neighbor and friend of Lisa Bailey in Alaska. Lisa and her friend had decided to leave Alaska and return to Lewis County. While the friend was waiting for Lisa to come and join her so they could leave Alaska together, she was listening to a police scanner and heard a call dispatched to the trailer park where Lisa was living. Lisa Bailey's death was ruled a suicide by the Alaska Troopers. Several years after Lisa's death, I spoke with the officers involved in her case. Sadly, enough time had elapsed that all the evidence in the "suicide case" had been destroyed.

In August of 2005, Bruce Kimsey and I went to Craig, Alaska, seeking any information we could find regarding the

Maurin homicides. One of the people we interviewed was Jim See, the Chief of Police in Craig. The chief looked for photos regarding Lisa Bailey's death, and it was determined that these photos had been sent to the Alaska Troopers. We also interviewed Naida, who lived in the same trailer park as Lisa and was her friend. She said that on the night of Lisa's death, she had been summoned to the trailer and observed her friend dead with a handgun in her hand. She recalled that the police had to restrain John Riffe because he was distraught and did not want anyone to touch Lisa. Naida recalled that her good friend Lisa was more drunk than usual the night she died. She also remembered that Lisa always acted like she was holding something over John's head. Lisa even told her one time, "If he ever does something to me, I can really hurt him."

Although our trip to Alaska involved a number of interviews with law enforcement and friends of Lisa and the Riffes, nothing particularly helpful came from our efforts. One of the more memorable incidents from the trip was the fact that the airline had lost my luggage. On the plane trip up, I was wearing a pair of aqua-colored scrub pants that were particularly comfortable for an aging fat guy. That ended up being the only pair of pants I had during this entire excursion. I was interviewing loggers, commercial fishermen, and cops in my aqua-colored scrub pants. Of course, Bruce Kimsey got photos of me in these pants, and

283

for the next several years, he called me "aqua man." Over the following years, he always showed a photo of me in my scrub pants at a number of different settings, including police conferences.

This case languished for several years until a new prosecutor was elected in Lewis County. This new official helped significantly. Bruce located another witness named Janice Hadaller, and she aided our investigation in a couple of unique ways. Janice was the niece of Minnie Hadaller, and she was able to pick John Riffe out of a "mug throw down." Apparently, she had made this same identification of the suspect in 1985, but that information was not known during the time of my active investigation.

When Bruce conducted the "mug throw down" with Janice in April of 2010, she was shown six photos. When she turned to the second photo, she said, "That's him, that's him! This was the man that I saw at Aunt Minnie's house the day I drove by with my sister." She also said that this was the man she had seen darting across the road from East to West at Yard Birds. Her first reference was from the day that Minnie and Ed were kidnapped. The second reference was from activity seen at Yard Birds, where the Maurin vehicle was dumped after the murders. Janice picked John Riffe's photo from the mug shots for both of these incidents. Janice Hadaller had grown up in the Mossy Rock area, but she had

284

never met the Riffe brothers. Bruce met Janice at Ed and Minnie Hadaller's residence on April 16, 2010. Janice showed Bruce where she had seen the Maurin vehicle on that fateful day. She also showed him where she had seen John Riffe near the Maurin's mailbox. She told Bruce about a van she had seen around Mossy Rock over the years, and she identified who owned the van.

That same day in 2010, Janice met Bruce in the Sterling Savings Bank lot in Chehalis, where she had seen the Maurin vehicle on the day of the kidnapping. She did not think anything of it at the time. The day she saw the Maurin vehicle at the bank, she said it appeared to have hit the van in the parking lot as it was backing up. In retrospect, she thought the van at the bank was the same van that she had seen at her aunt Minnie's house earlier that day. From the bank, Janice and Bruce went to Yard Birds. Janice showed Bruce where she had seen the van and the man, identified as John Riffe, darting across the road near the vehicle. The takeaway from this two-fold identification of the car and one of the suspects was that the killers needed a ride away from the Maurin vehicle once they parked it.

After these interviews, Bruce returned to his office and found Janice's statements that were taken in 1986. They had not been followed up on after the Riffes were identified as likely suspects. Several months after the Janice Hadaller interviews, Bruce interviewed Marjorie Hadaller, who had been with Janice on the day of the murders. She told Bruce that she had never been interviewed by the police regarding this issue and confirmed that she was in the car with Janice when they drove by the Maurin home. She recalled seeing a man in the driveway but did not get a good look at his face as she was driving. She also recalled seeing a man at Yard Birds wearing dark clothing and carrying what was likely a rifle. Her story matched her sister Janice's story. The fact that Janice and Marjorie Hadaller's observations were not followed up on around the time of the homicide was unfortunate, to say the least.

After Bruce Kimsey obtained identification confirmation with the mug throw-downs, the case took on a new dimension and direction. An arrest warrant for murder was issued to Rick Riffe. We learned that John Gregory Riffe had recently died, or he would have been arrested for murder, as well as his brother Rick. In July 2012, a group of us flew to a small town on the beaten path named King Salmon, Alaska. Included in that group were Lewis County Deputy Prosecutor William Halstead, Alaska Trooper Bill Gifford, Detective Dan Riordan, Bruce Kimsey from Lewis County, and me.

Our first stop in town was at the Rent-a-Wreck car rental agency. The proprietor handed us several sets of keys and sent us to our cars. The battery was dead on one of the cars, and the female proprietor of this fine establishment became bothered by our presence in the office again. She begrudgingly handed us a pair of jumper cables and told us to jump our own battery. After getting a couple of cars rented, we drove by the Riffe family home on Wolverine Dr. We then introduced ourselves to the local cops and started preparing for the long overdue arrest of Rick Riffe. That night Bruce once again over-indulged in one of King Salmon's two bars, and we all had a good night in this very small, tight-knit community.

The next morning, while eating lunch in one of the two restaurants in town, we began talking amongst ourselves about the next step in the arrest of Rick Riffe. We had a pleasant conversation with our female waitress over the course of our meal. Fortunately, we did not include her in our discussions, as our waitress that day was Sherry Tibbetts. We would later find out that Tibbetts had been companions with Rick Riffe for twenty-two years, and the two lived together just a short distance from the restaurant.

The group of us arrived at the Riffe residence on Wolverine Dr at 4:45 p.m. on July 8, 2012. There were no police cars or uniformed officers in our group. Given the fact that I was no longer a police detective, I decided that I did not want to be armed during our visit to the Riffe residence.

For this reason, I kept a low profile at the initial stages of this long-awaited event. It had been almost twenty-seven years since the Maurins were brutally murdered.

Alaska Trooper Bill Gifford knocked on the door several times, and there was no answer. Finally, Rick Riffe came to the door and invited us in after we identified ourselves. Bruce asked Riffe if he would come to the trooper's office, but he did not want to go with us. Bruce and I proceeded to interview Rick Riffe. At this point in my career, I had been conducting serious interviews for over forty years. Bruce had not been involved as long as me, but he had significant experience and was good at his chosen career. Riffe had likely been expecting this interview for the previous twenty-seven years.

Bruce and I were familiar with the Riffe brothers and their associates over the years since the homicides. We both asked questions and took notes. Many of our questions were about people whom we had already spoken with and what they had told us about the events immediately following the murders. Rick's response was often, "I don't remember." Rick's ex-wife Robin Riffe had told friends that her husband had killed the Maurins. When confronted with this statement, Rick said Robin was just trying to get him. Unfortunately for us, Robin was no longer alive. One of Rick's former girlfriends, whom I had interviewed previously, told me that Rick had terrorized one of her children with a tarantula. We asked him if he had ever owned a tarantula, and he said that he had.

When asked, Rick said that he and Robin Riffe had broken up in 1986 or 1987. We told him that Robin had a clear recognition of the crime scene where the Maurins' bodies had been found. He was then asked where Robin could have come up with that information, and he, of course, had no idea. We asked him about going to the area of White Pass with Robin to buy two ounces of cocaine from Ralph Vickers in December of 1985. He recalled that trip and said he went with Robin, as she was really the dope dealer. He did not, however, recall buying as much as two ounces. This was helpful as a significant amount of money had changed hands during this transaction, and Vickers had verified the story to us previously. Rick was also asked if he had cut off the barrel of a 12 gauge shotgun for Les George. He recalled doing that for his friend Les, but he could not recall why he had done so. This was likely the gun used to kill the Maurins.

We asked questions and spoke with Rick for about two hours. It was apparent that the questioning was not going anywhere. Rick was calm and did not get unpleasant with us. He never made any effort to escape or be confrontational. Part of this was likely attributed to the fact that he was using an oxygen machine during the interview. Rick was then transported to the local police station and processed for murder, kidnapping, and robbery. While Bruce and I were still at the police station, we learned that our waitress from earlier that day, Sherry Tibbetts, was also there hoping to speak with us. We spoke with Sherry and her son for twenty to thirty minutes. She was distraught and told us that Rick had been a good role model for her sons for the past twenty-two years.

The news of Rick Riffe's arrest was a significant event in Lewis County. The headline in the local paper was: "Suspect Arrested in the 1985 slaying of Lewis County Couple." The Sheriff of Lewis County at that time was Steve Mansfield, and his quote in the local paper was as follows: "It is through the tenacious, patient, and diligent work of Detective Bruce Kimsey, Private Investigator Chris Peterson, the Prosecuting Attorney's Office, and Ed and Minnie Maurin's son Dennis Hadaller that this day has finally come. The Maurin/ Hadaller families suffered a horrific and tragic loss of their family members and now will be able to see justice served."

Approximately eighteen months later, in November of 2013, a trial was held in Lewis County, and Rick Riffe was found guilty of murder, kidnapping, first-degree robbery, and burglary. The jury deliberated for a day and a half. A special relationship developed between myself, Dennis

Hadaller, who hired me, and Bruce Kimsey, the great detective who brought this ugly case to its final end. I'd like to say a quick word about my friend Bruce Kimsey. Bruce is a large guy with a big black mustache. He is thirty years younger than I am, and he could sell ice to an Eskimo. Evidence of his sales ability became apparent to me on our first trip to Alaska at a bar in Ketchikan. Bruce had over-indulged a bit, but I did not, as I was drinking some kind of herbal tea. Anyway, Bruce convinced several patrons in the bar that I had been a famous jockey at one time. That was a great tall tale full of bullshit, as I weighed two-hundred-and-fifty pounds and stood six feet tall. Bruce was an army veteran who had spent time in Kosovo sleeping in armored personnel carriers in the cold. I was never able to get verification on that, so we will just put this story in the unverified category. All of these stories are likely one of the reasons I call Bruce my "bastard son." When I first met Bruce, he told me that while he was watching *COPS* as a young kid, he saw me on TV. Years later, when we met, he brought up that story immediately, and we quickly became friends.

Maurin Murders - Bruce Kimsey, Lewis County Sheriff Detective with Dennis Hadaller, son of the victims.

CHIEF

The next story has a lot of personal meaning to me. My parents were divorced when I was five years old. I ended up living with my father and did not see my mother a lot when I was growing up. My mom Tina was remarried to a remarkable guy named Don Prophet. When he was a young marine, Don lost the use of his right arm in the South Pacific during World War II. Consequently, he spent a long time in a military hospital recovering from his wounds. Don had very little formal education, as he had gone into the marines right out of high school. When he was finally able to go back to work, he was employed as a janitor at Mountain Home Air

292

Force Base in Idaho. Although he was essentially a one-armed janitor, after several years of employment, Don was the top civilian in the base's supply operation.

As I understand it, most of the marines in Don's company died in combat. There were three that survived with significant injuries. One of the survivors was Jim Phillips, and he and his wife stayed in touch with my mom and Don. Jim had a long career with the Caterpillar Corporation in Bloomington, Illinois. Jim, Don, and my mom spent years trying to find "Chief." He was the third survivor from their marine company, and his name was George Adams. I had heard about the search for "Chief" over the years and found it interesting, but I was busy with my police career and never got involved.

My stepdad, Don, passed away in 1971. His death was likely related to his wartime injuries. For some inexplicable reason, I stayed in touch with Jim Phillips, and I met with him and his wife on several occasions. We would talk every six months or so on the phone, and the topic of "Chief" always seemed to come up. One day Jim and I were talking on the phone, and the topic came up again. Something told me it was time to get involved in the search for "Chief." At this point in time, Jim knew that I was a private investigator. We talked about my potential involvement, and he quickly said, "I will pay you!" I recalled a photo of Jim on a South

Pacific island during the war with his arm in a sling and told him he had already paid the bill for his service to our country.

Jim thought that George was from Southern Arizona, but he wasn't sure what tribe he was from. I did some research, and we ultimately believed that George was from the Tohono O'odham Nation. This nation covers about four-thousand-four-hundred-and-sixty square miles, which is roughly the size of Connecticut. I started out by running George's name in a commercial database. I had no firm idea where George lived in regard to a state or city. I suspected Arizona was likely the state, but other than that, I was unsure. George Adams was also a very common name that presented a problem, although we did know a general age range that ruled out several people. The commercial database proved to be of no help. Indian Nations have their own law enforcement agencies and are not tied into many of the usual state networks that most private investigators are familiar with.

I called the Tohono O'odham Nation Tribal Police and was candid with them about my motives for finding George Adams. They did not have anything helpful to add except for the name of the postmistress in Sells, AZ. I called the lady and explained to her why I was looking for George. She said she did not know him, but she might know a family member. That family member eventually called me and identified who

George Adams was. The family member no longer lived on the reservation, but she told me who George's ninety-year-old brother was and gave me the basic location of his house. Addresses did not seem to be a big part of direction finding in Sells.

I found George's brother, and he quickly took me to the deserted adobe shack out in the desert where George had grown up. He then took me to a cemetery out in the same area and showed me George's grave. There were two or three other graves nearby, but it was isolated. There was a community cemetery several hundred yards away. Near the community cemetery, there were numerous signs warning about rattlesnakes. For some reason, it had taken the family many years to get the headstone that military members are entitled to. George's new headstone read that he was born June 22, 1922, and died June 9, 1994. I gave George a snappy salute with tears in my eyes and went away.

I was saddened by the fact that George was no longer with us but heartened that I could pass this information on to one of America's heroes, Jim Phillips. I quickly sent the photos to Jim. I had solved a mystery that was important to many people in my life, and Jim was overjoyed. It was not long before Jim was in Sells, Arizona, looking to find his long-lost friend. Jim was with his daughter Carol and her husband, Don Munson. I got a call from Jim, and they could not find George's grave. I had made notes about the location, but given the lack of addresses and street names, it was a problem. I told them that I would get on a plane and come down immediately if that would help. They said not to worry and told me that they would try the next day again.

Jim Phillips at "Chief's" grave near Sells Arizona on the reservation.

The following day the group of three was back out in the desert looking for George. They were approached by a female border patrol agent who told them that they were on tribal lands and should not be there. She said that the area was dangerous, as it was close to the Mexican border and part of a pathway for smugglers involved in illicit activities. Jim Phillips told the agent why he was there. As it turned out, she had recently been discharged from the marine corps. She respectfully told Jim and his family to take all the time they needed. A few days later, I received a photo of Jim standing proudly with his right hand on George Adam's headstone. This was one of my greatest investigative achievements.

STOLEN PROPERTY: RUSSIAN SURPRISE

One of my more interesting P.I. cases involved a Vancouver, Washington, company that was in the exercise equipment business. I was contacted by their legal counsel in March 2016, and I met with them at their office on the 21st of March. An astute paralegal had noticed that a high volume of their equipment was being sold regularly on computer websites like Craigslist. The paralegal had compiled phone numbers and the types of equipment that were being advertised on "the black market." After looking over the company's warehouse, I determined that the camera security system needed a major upgrade, so I made arrangements to get that done. It was necessary to keep the camera work undisclosed, as we really did not know who was involved within the company. The work was kept quiet except for a few trusted employees and had to be done when there were no workers around. We got the covert cameras installed thanks to one of the real experts, Mike Hansen.

The warehouse was a large building, and it offered some surveillance challenges. It was very isolated and difficult to observe warehouse activities without being seen by potential suspects. In fact, some of the employees did notice my surveillance guys working in the area. At one point, a man and woman confronted one of my guys pretty aggressively and wanted to know what he was doing. We had suspicions that the man and woman had grown concerned that we were watching them for reasons unrelated to theft. One of these people actually went to the company management and expressed concerns about what he had seen. Management contacted me, and we discussed the developing issue. I was able to convince them that we could still proceed. We amassed many surveillance videos and photos showing the property being removed from the warehouse. We had a good idea of who was fencing the bulk of the stolen property and knew that he lived in Vancouver, WA. Through surveillance, we saw a fair number of deliveries to his house by company employees and had witnessed him selling and delivering stolen property around the Portland Metro area.

At this point in my P.I. career, I was connected with a cadre of world-class investigators with a number of specialized skills. One of the subsets was with general investigators, and another one was with surveillance detectives. Some folks do both of these processes well, while others are good at either one or the other. I did five to six years of constant surveillance as a police detective. I thought that I was very good at it and just knew that it would be a piece of cake as a P.I. I was wrong in assuming this fact, though. As a P.I., I suddenly did not have five or more guys assisting me in every surveillance, often with the use of an airplane as well. Generally speaking, doing mobile surveillance as a cop involved a number of cars. If one got spotted, you just told someone else to take the lead as you dropped out of sight.

In fairness to the cop's side of this, we were often following dope dealers or other serious offenders who were always watching their rear-view mirror. This same group of folks would often rent homes on dead-end streets, so they could see what vehicles were in their area. As a P.I., the average client did not want to pay for multiple surveillance vehicles. In the equipment theft case, however, the company was happy to allow me to use multiple operatives. After the case had gone on for two months, though, there were corporate concerns that we were spending significant amounts of money with questionable results.

As I worked on this case, I was using some P.I.s who had years of experience working alone. Some had been cops, and some had not. As I look back on this case, I used eight to nine operatives regularly who likely had over two hundred cumulative years of experience. We had obtained lots of photographic evidence and were moving in the right direction. On May 27, 2016, I got a call from the paralegal who had been periodically monitoring the camera activity at the warehouse when it was closed. She said, "We got them." I asked whom we got, and she named one of the employees, Lester Ambers, who had entered the warehouse with an unknown person. They had then loaded up a white pickup and a large white trailer with equipment and departed the area.

Several hours earlier, I had my former police partner Bob Peterson reach out to a Craigslist post advertising equipment for sale that we believed was stolen. Bobbie made contact with the Craigslist seller and was directed to come to 6819 SE 65th Ave. in Portland. This was in the district that I had cut my teeth on as a rookie cop, the one that we lovingly called Squirrel Heights or Felony Flats. Bobbie went to the address and purchased dumbbells from a person later identified as Pavel Sabadash. Bobbie had arrived at the Sabadash house at 5:20 p.m. and bought a set of dumbbells for $250. While making this purchase, he saw boxes of products sitting on the front porch that was likely stolen from our client.

A short time after Bobbie left the house, he saw an email I had sent out prior to his visit to the house. The Email included a photo of the pickup and trailer that had been obtained by the security camera at the warehouse. My Email said, "Guys, take a look at this trailer and keep it in mind as we make buys. We think this is the same trailer that went into the warehouse a few weeks ago and left with weights. It looks like it has OR plates on it.... Bob P, pay special attention to the Squirrel location. Pretty unique trailer...." As soon as Bobbie saw my Email with the photos, he called me into the office and said, "I just left that trailer at the 65th Ave. house." I was elated, as it seemed that the big break we had been hoping for had just presented itself.

I immediately called the paralegal and told her to call the Portland Police and have them make contact with Det. Bob Peterson. Bobbie was now watching the 65th Ave. house with Ralph Radmer, a P.I. and highly regarded, retired Portland detective. Ralph and I had been classmates in the police academy. This incident was now coming full circle, combining my life as a P.I. with my earlier career in law enforcement.

A Portland Police officer made contact with Bobbie and Ralph, and he was briefed on what we knew and didn't know about the situation. At that moment, we did not know the name of the suspect. The paralegal had identified the employee thief as Lester Ambers, who was the warehouse manager. The Portland uniformed officer had a cover car with him, and they went to the 65th Ave. house where the offending pickup and trailer were parked. As it turned out, the primary Portland officer responding spoke Russian, as did Sabadash. Bobbie had briefed the Portland officer about his recent purchase of the stolen warehouse items, and the officer contacted Sabadash asking him where he had obtained the exercise equipment. He said that he got it from a guy and had picked the equipment up at a warehouse in NE Portland.

About this time, a woman believed to be Sabadash's wife came out and started yelling at him in Russian. This woman did not like the person her husband had been dealing with, and she made several incriminating statements in Russian. This incident was quite fortuitous, as the Portland police officer who spoke Russian heard the statements and realized how helpful they were. Guilt had essentially been admitted before any real questions were asked.

The Portland officer showed Sabadash the photos of his truck and trailer at the warehouse. The officer asked him if he could look inside the trailer, so Sabadash unlocked the compartment, which was now empty. The officer asked him where the equipment was, as the warehouse camera had photos of the equipment being loaded into the trailer. Sabadash said he did not know what the officer was talking about. He was then told that we had a video of the stolen equipment being loaded into the trailer. At that point, Sabadash started quickly walking away, but he was immediately placed in handcuffs and put into the back seat of the police car. Once Sabadash realized that we had a solid case against him, he decided to cooperate. He said that he had purchased the equipment from a man named Lester but did not know his last name. He knew where Lester lived in Vancouver and also knew that he worked at the warehouse where the equipment had come from in NE Portland.

Sabadash said he initially met Lester through a Craigslist ad and that he had made a number of exercise equipment purchases from him over a period of six months. Sabadash said he had paid $9,000 for the load of merchandise that he had picked up today. He allowed the officer to examine his phone, and it appeared that there had been at least twenty-seven previous transactions between the two men. Sabadash realized that our case was solid, and he soon showed officers where all the stolen property was stored at his home.

During all this, I had been sitting in my office "directing traffic," orchestrating all of these activities over the radio and via cell phone. As it turned out, Sabadash had a retail value of $50,000 in stolen property on his premises. I called my paralegal contact and made arrangements for the company to send one of their large trucks to the "Squirrel" address so that we could return the property to the possession of its rightful owner. This was May 28, 2016, and it was the beginning of Memorial Day weekend. Most everyone working for me at the moment had plans for the holiday that did not include filling up a large truck with heavy items. I told everyone that we would raise the hourly rate considerably if they stayed and helped, so they did. Six months later, in January of 2017, Lester Ambers was sentenced to eighteen months in prison after pleading guilty to Theft 1. He was also ordered to pay $198,000 in restitution.

We were aware that another person had also been receiving significant amounts of stolen equipment. His name was Roman White, and he lived in Vancouver. He had been handling numerous items of stolen property that were being delivered to him by another employee of the same company. We had taken photos of equipment boxes that had been unloaded in his yard. At one point, we watched White take empty boxes that had contained stolen equipment to a recycling center. We had an investigator go to the recycling center and recover the boxes for evidentiary purposes.

Our video surveillance of White showed that he was making deliveries of the stolen property around the metro area. We also knew that he and his wife were selling these items on Craigslist. On May 28th, we had one of our investigators place an order via Craigslist for an expensive item. The day before that, we had recovered a significant amount of stolen items and were concerned that larger amounts of property may disappear from White if we did not act quickly. Mike Franks, working on my behalf, made arrangements to meet Roman White in a Fred Meyers' parking lot in Vancouver. We were concerned that word may have leaked about our activities from the day earlier. Mike and I were watching closely to see if we could observe any counter-surveillance in the area. At one point in time, we thought that we did, so I left the area for a few minutes.

Subsequently, Mike purchased a new piece of equipment still in the box for $1500. The retail price on it was $4,000. Roman told Mike that he had a lot of equipment available at good prices. White had apparently not heard about the major event from the day before, where we had seized the equipment from Sabadash. We turned over huge amounts of information and evidence to the Clark County Sheriff's Office as well as the legal counsel who had hired us.

305

Segments of our investigation were handled civilly, and other parts were handled criminally.

My investigative world has intersected with my previous police career in many interesting ways. One of the first police officers I got to know in the Portland area was Les Frank, who was Mike Franks' stepfather. Les was an Oregon State Trooper, and I probably met him in 1972. Forty-two years later, I found myself working a stolen property case with the son of a great friend. This particular case was solved by some of the best P.I. s in the area, many of whom were retired from Multnomah County Sheriff's Office, Portland Police Department, San Jose P.D., Gresham P.D., and Elko, NV P.D. All of these retired guys had extensive experience in criminal investigations.

Out of respect for my former police partner, Bob Peterson, I have to make the following comment. Bobbie was the most incredible undercover person I have ever worked with. When he got involved in this particular case, my blood pressure dropped to a good level. On this day in 2016, Bobbie was my partner again, just like we had been in the '80s and '90s. To say that Bobbie was quite self-assured would be an understatement. When Bobbie passed away in 2021, many of us lost a great friend, a family member, and one of the world's best investigators.

ANOTHER "BOBBIE" STORY

Bobbie retired several years after I did. As soon as he got his P.I. license, I started giving him cases to work on. The following are a few of the many Bobbie and Chris P.I. cases for some fun insight. One of them was a job that required a significant amount of surveillance in a casino near Pendleton, OR. Bobbie went there a couple of times and spent several days at a time. This was a number of years ago. I told him I would pay all expenses and said I would even pay him $50 a day for gambling expenses, as the observations needed to be made in the casino. He made two trips and was successful on both of them. Several months after the job was completed, he laughingly confessed to me that he didn't really make any money on that case because he lost a lot in the casino. Bobbie, Bobbie, Bobbie.

Right after Bobbie retired from the Gresham Police Department, I was hired by a woman who was being severely harassed by an ex-husband. She lived in Vancouver, and I was able to locate her ex in Portland. The clown was sending her nasty and offensive mail. He also left a bag of human waste on the woman's porch and did other petty things to her as well. When a neighbor's security camera picked up the suspect's van, the victim went to the police to complain. The police, unfortunately, could not help her with what she needed, which was to get this asshole to

307

leave her alone. The ex was a bit elusive, but I was finally able to locate him.

I called Bobbie and asked him to assist, as I was not sure what I would encounter when I finally located this fool. It was time for Bobbie and Chris to reunite in the battle against evil. I told Bobbie to meet me at the address at about noon. He did, and of course, our friend was not home. We went to lunch at a nearby restaurant and returned to the suspect's house a bit later, but he still wasn't home. It was as if no time had passed at all, as Bobbie and I were doing surveillance together again like we had done hundreds of times before. Sitting a block away, waiting for the bad guy to show up, we shot the breeze about everything under the sun except for politics: that was a forbidden subject on stakeouts.

The idiot finally arrived home an hour later and parked his van. It appeared that he was unloading groceries. We quickly joined him by his back door. I explained that I was doing some work for a woman in Vancouver who was being severely harassed. I asked him several different ways if he was involved in anything similar. Of course, his answer was, "No." We went on for several minutes, but I never mentioned my client's name during this conversation.

I told this doofus that his van was seen in the area where the problem had occurred, and of course, he said he was never at that location with his van. We played the fish for a while, and then one of us said, "Do you ever loan that van out?" His initial reaction was, "No." Then he saw an opening to get out of his lie and said, "Yeah, I did loan it out one time." This was when the Bobbie and Chris symphony started. It was like we had never quit working together. Both of us started in on the man, and it went like this: "You need to tell that stupid son of a bitch whom you loaned the van to knock that shit off. He must be a really ignorant asshole, and he is going to cause you a lot of trouble." This berating went on for a couple of minutes, and then it was time for us to leave. We met down the street a couple of blocks and did the Peterson brother's high-five before heading our separate ways. I always enjoyed my time working with Bob Peterson during my years as a law enforcement officer and later as a private investigator.

Chapter 16

O.W.L.A. - OREGON WASHINGTON LAWMEN'S ASSOCIATION

In 1958, a multi-agency training organization named the Oregon Washington Lawmen's Association (O.W.L.A.) was formed in Oregon and Washington. One of the founders of this organization was Myron Warren, who was a Portland Police Officer. Myron rose through the ranks during his distinguished career, and I had the good fortune of getting acquainted with him. After Myron retired from law enforcement, he held a number of significant jobs in the security field. One of his jobs was the director of security for Tektronix. As a Multnomah County Detective, I had an opportunity to work with Myron on a case in which Tektronix was losing gold that was a by-product of their circuit board production. It was a pleasure to have Myron as a mentor for many years.

The original intent of the O.W.L.A. was to facilitate the timely exchange of information regarding safecrackers. This was before the time of good alarm systems, security cameras, texting of photos, and good police radio systems. Before modern alarm systems came into play, safecracking was a significant problem. The original board members of the O.W.L.A. were officers from Multnomah County,

Portland, OR; Aberdeen, WA; Beaverton, OR; Camas, WA; Bingen, WA; and the Portland Parks Department. O.W.L.A. soon became a valuable tool for the development of professionalism and networking for law enforcement. One of the first presenters I heard from was Paul Groza, who was a Portland Postal Inspector. Paul was helpful to me many times in the ensuing years.

During my police career and my second career as a private investigator, I received world-class training on every type of crime one can imagine. O.W.L.A. charged a small fee for attending their conferences. With the help of good secretaries and treasurers, the organization did a great job ensuring there were adequate funds to bring in the "best of the best" for presentations. The organization brought law enforcement experts in from all over the country as presenters, including officers from Oregon, Washington, L.A.P.D., the Texas Rangers, the D.E.A., and the F.B.I., to name a few. This was all thanks to Myron Warren and the other founders of the Oregon Washington Lawmen's Association.

I had the good fortune of being asked to join the O.W.L.A. as a board member in the mid-90s, and I served in that role for the next thirty years. Several of my police partners from Multnomah County served as president of this great group, including Rod Englert, Jim McNelly, and Keith

Krafve. Being a part of O.W.L.A. was truly a gift to me and my career. I became friends and colleagues with hundreds of folks ranging from chiefs and sheriffs to rookie detectives. I was able to see law enforcement officers who were active from the 1950s through the 2020s. The bond among police officers is an unusual one that few people ever experience.

In 2016, I was on my way to interview a convict who was housed in a pen at McNeil Island, WA. The city of Lacy was nearby, so I decided to stop in at Lacy P.D. I knew my friend Larry Dickerson, the Lacy Chief of Police, was within a week of retirement. He had been president of the O.W.L.A. at one time. I spent an hour visiting with Larry. You would have thought that I was attending a funeral. Everyone that I saw appeared to be on the verge of tears. This is the bond of law enforcement officers that I have referred to many times in this book.

Epilogue

As I am putting the finishing touches on this story, I have huge concerns. My grandad was a true American pioneer. My father was part of the greatest generation. My teachers throughout my young life all appeared to love America, as did my family members who raised me and taught me a lot of important values. To say that I was well-to-do growing up would be inaccurate. When I was thirteen or fourteen years old, I remember leaving change lying around the house. I did this so that my father would pick it up and use it, as I knew we were poor. At least, that is what I thought, so I always managed to find a part-time job to earn money.

As I reach the golden years, I live very comfortably. I am surrounded by my burros, my dogs, my horse, my trees, and my loving family. No one handed me anything, and I worked into my late 70's. My concerns today are about the country that I grew up in. I spent twenty-six years working to keep Portland the beautiful and enjoyable city that many of us loved. Today I avoid going to Portland as I fear crime and do not want to see the filth that is everywhere.

A part of this problem involves my brothers and sisters in law enforcement. Their current-day numbers have dwindled to dangerously low levels. They do not have the support of some prosecutors or many of the city's leaders.

They are required to deal with lawlessness that no cops in the past one hundred years have had to put up with. If they overreact when mobs destroy the city, they have to be concerned about lawsuits and a lack of support from the government. Laws throughout the country are being changed to take away legitimate tools that cops have had for years.

On a sad note, who would really want to be a cop today when you could find yourself a high-tech job and work from home? Normally in that environment, at least no one is throwing bags of shit at you. There are all kinds of dangerous jobs, some more perilous than law enforcement. The difference is that in those more dangerous jobs, no one is really trying to kill you. If we do not get behind our cops and support them, we may end up with a bunch of officers that we don't really want to do the job. You do not have to look too far to see that type of scenario in action. Simply look at much of the world South of our border. In Mexico, the pay for police officers is poor, and no one trusts the cops. Everything is for sale.

In these previous chapters, I have provided a snapshot of some of the cases that I worked on as a patrol officer, a dope cop, a detective, and a private investigator. It has been very interesting, to say the least. Looking back on my law enforcement career, there were a few little cases that made me proud. One of them involved a grandmother whose silverware was taken in a burglary; I got the silverware back for her when I arrested the burglar. There was the retiree who created a makeshift alarm by tying aluminum cans together with a fishing line so that when someone came over his fence, all the cans would fall and alert him. I eventually arrested the burglar who made this blue-collar retiree afraid to leave his wife alone at home to go fishing. There was my first detective case where I arrested a person for robbery who had simply snatched a six-pack of beer and run out of a convenience store. He had used force on the clerk, which resulted in the charge being a robbery.

One night Deputy Carl McDade and I were working in uniform in Squirrel Heights. There was a large beer party in the neighborhood. We weren't particularly interested in the party, but we were looking for a wanted person that we had reason to think would be in attendance. We had parked our prowl car several blocks away and were hiding in the weeds watching for our wanted friend. We were near a bus stop on SE Flavel St. when we saw a man walk up and hit the lone man waiting for his bus with a chain several times. The victim of this assault was mentally challenged, and he was being beaten just so the criminal could steal his portable radio.

I could go on for pages in this regard. None of these cases made the 10:00 p.m. news. I did not get an "attaboy" for any of these cases or arrests. I did not get a pay raise for any of this. I was not much different than all of the folks I worked with. The bulk of us wanted the community that paid us to be a safer place. The folks that paid our wages could call 911 and expect to see us in person, wearing a gold badge, and carrying a gun that was not a decorative piece.

In these modern times, the U.S. has become lawless in many of the major metropolitan areas. Cops have become the bad guys in the eyes of much of the public. There is the occasional police officer who makes a terrible decision or a series of bad decisions. We do not need that police officer. There are doctors, attorneys, teachers, counselors, nurses, truck drivers, and so on who make terrible decisions. We need to get rid of these bad seeds when we can, but don't demonize the entire group for the sins of the few. Cops can't change what is happening in the country. The changes can only be made by politicians, prosecutors, and taxpayers. Legislators in many states have decriminalized a lot of bad behavior. They have made it nearly impossible to protect the community in the way that my colleagues and I were proudly able to do in the past. Due to many terrible legislative decisions, what was once a felony has often been reduced to a misdemeanor. Crackpot D.A. s are not charging many minor crimes. Thus we have gangs of thugs going into stores and cleaning them out with little or no fear of prosecution.

When I left the air force as a captain, I took a significant pay cut to become a police officer. I spent some time in the Portland area during my freshman year of college. As a result of that experience, I fell in love with the city. We had Mt. Hood, two large rivers, tree-covered hills, beautiful city parks, a lot of nice people, and hundreds of great restaurants. I spent years 'warming the pines' in the hallways of the Multnomah County Courthouse, waiting to testify. The courthouse was surrounded by great coffee shops, delis, and fun night spots. Today downtown Portland is a social desert. I recently needed to go to a law office in that area. It was in a nice high-rise building, but I couldn't even find the entrance, as the entire first floor of windows was covered by plywood. The city I have grown to love over the course of my career as a police officer and private investigator is virtually unrecognizable today.

This story started when I was lying in my yard in Clarkston, Washington. I had just graduated from high school and thought I was all grown up. I remember wondering what I would do for a living and thinking, "Whatever it is, I hope it is interesting." Looking back now, to say it was interesting is an understatement.

"It was interesting"

CPSIA information can be obtained
at www.ICGtesting.com
Printed in the USA
BVHW091322260123
657211BV00010B/154